GETTING TO AHA!

getting to
aha!

WHY TODAY'S INSIGHTS ARE TOMORROW'S FACTS

DARSHAN MEHTA

LIONCREST
PUBLISHING

GETTING TO AHA!
Why Today's Insights Are Tomorrow's Facts

ISBN   978-1-61961-772-8 *Paperback*
       978-1-61961-773-5 *Ebook*

To the renegades, pioneers, and rebels who strive to make a difference.

CONTENTS

INTRODUCTION..........9

1. BRANDING AND HUMAN NATURE.......... 21

2. INSIGHTS....................57

3. DIGITAL VS. BIZ........................ 81

4. THE ERA OF EXPERIENCES 99

5. THE ERA OF BLENDING..........................111

6. THE ERA OF (NOT) THINKING 121

7. AHA! MOMENTS...................... 135

8. THE DIGITAL PROMISE 151

CONCLUSION...........................161

ACKNOWLEDGMENTS 167

ABOUT THE AUTHOR..............................169

INTRODUCTION

The best vision is insight.

MALCOLM FORBES

In today's world, whether you're a fledgling startup or an established brand, you're operating in a world of hyper-competition. Whatever products or services you sell, you're up against not only the company down the street but also the one across the state, the one across the country, and the one halfway around the world. Technology gives you new opportunities to deliver products and services at scale, globalizing customer access and minimizing barriers to entry for passionate, disruptive entrepreneurs. Today, brands must carve out positions they can own and defend. They must differentiate themselves from their peers to establish strong emotional connections with their customer base. This is a daunting proposition for young startups. But successful brands know and speak to their audiences. Companies that understand their customers' needs, fears, desires, and problems—and what they are willing to pay to fix them—will survive. But those that chase insights—and put them to use—will *thrive*.

This book is about acquiring these insights. It's a guide to the tools entrepreneurs, marketers, and everyday individuals can use to uncover them. But more importantly, it's about uncovering and interpreting the cultural trends that make these insights all the more powerful.

Arriving at insights is both a science and an art. And ultimately, it relies on the one elusive constant technology that remains hard-pressed to replicate or replace: humanity.

CHASING INSIGHTS: THE TOOLS AT YOUR DISPOSAL

I've been working as a brand strategist and marketing researcher for more than 15 years. I help clients figure out what ultimately drives consumers to buy their product or service—the *why* behind customers' decision-making processes.

As we'll discuss in detail in chapter two, I've come to realize that insights are multidimensional. They incorporate not only quantitative data but also a deep understanding of consumers' needs and desires. They speak to the societal trends influencing consumers' purchasing habits and brand sentiments.

Fortunately, technology has made it easier than ever to square insights' quantitative and qualitative components. With just a few clicks, these new tools can track responses to advertising, map website behavior, conduct digital surveys, compile audience trends, and much more.

But while quantitative data is inarguably useful in business, it can't offer a true picture of consumer behavior. It delivers the *what* but rarely the *why*.

To get a firm grip on your customers' purchase decision-making behavior, you must pair quantitative data with its *qualitative* counterpart. These non-numerical assessments can take you to the emotional heart of consumers' decision making—to the *why*. And the ideal vehicle of qualitative data? Genuine, human-to-human conversation.

THE LOST ART OF CONVERSATION

Mastering the art of customer conversation begins with this realization: you're going to hear from your patrons whether you want to or not. If you're a bar, restaurant, or café, they'll review you on Yelp. If you're a hotel or resort, they'll talk about you on TripAdvisor. Whether you're a clothing retailer, a consumer products manufacturer, a technology platform, or even a health-care facility, your fans and detractors will plaster their thoughts about you across any number of channels, including Facebook, Twitter, Instagram, and an ever-growing number of specialized sites and blogs.

Your customers will do all of this without warning and without your permission. Whether you invite it or not, you *are* going to hear from your customers.

The only way to deal with this is head-on. Engage your customers where they are. Understand their grievances so that you may limit future ones. Ask what drives them nuts about your product and brand. Listen when they tell you, "I really hate it when X breaks down, and I have to keep fixing it," or "I can't believe I have to hold this button down with my right hand in order to turn on this machine with my left." Your customers may not know how you can solve their problems, but they'll happily tell you what those problems are.

Engaging with negative feedback can be easier said than done. But there are two rules to remember. The first is that negativity happens. Not everyone is going to love your product or service; no matter what you do, you won't make everyone happy. The second is that negativity itself matters less than your response to it—and you must respond to it. Leaving unfavorable comments unaddressed allows them to become "facts," while sharing thoughtful, genuine responses can mitigate the impact of negative ones. Your customers understand that "s*@! happens," and they'll appreciate your responsiveness and willingness to own up to a mistake.

Positive or negative, addressed or not, customer feedback is out there. Businesses that enter into exchanges with their fans and detractors alike are those that pull critical insights into reach. They are the companies that constantly challenge themselves to deliver the experience their customers want, refining their products and services and differentiating themselves from their competitors.

At the end of the day, your brand can only be validated by its customers—not by you. You control the product or service you offer, your mission and values, and your customer communications. But only your customers can appreciate your product, mission, values, and communication. It's a synergistic relationship. And the way to build a maximally productive one is to get to know your audience through conversations.

WHAT *ARE* INSIGHTS ANYWAY?

When I talk to people about insights, I often realize that

they don't truly understand what insights are. Many understand insights as simple observations or facts. But insights are multidimensional. They're combinations of observations *and* facts, influenced by overarching socio-cultural and technological trends that make us say "*aha!*" Recognizing insights requires us to venture beyond our comfort zones—to consider ideas and situations from fresh perspectives, believe insights are out there waiting to be uncovered, and trust that today's insights are tomorrow's facts.

Consider the example of fonts. We exercise our creativity in the fonts we use to write everything from essays to blog posts to marketing copy to books like this one. We take these choices for granted. But when the first generation of personal computers came to market, IBM and leading software developers used only a handful of fonts. Developers and marketers paid scant attention to the fact that consumers may want something more stylized. Around this time, Steve Jobs was taking calligraphy classes at Reed College. Jobs saw the functionality of personal computers (a fact) and our impending dependency on them (a trend), and he combined these with his observations about humans' emotional attachment to art and design.

Once upon a time, the idea that our experiences and product choice could be influenced by font design was an insight. Now, it's a fact, and it's driving innovation at tech companies ranging in size from startups to Apple.

EXERCISING EMPATHY

When you're chasing insights, it's important to remember that arriving at them requires a deep understanding of human behavior. You need to be curious and inquisitive. You need to ask questions and listen carefully to answers. And you need to have empathy. How do those qualities lead to insights? Here's an example. I've been teaching executives how to deliver business presentations for many years. I've done this in North America, Europe, and Asia. In one popular exercise, I ask participants to persuade a group of Midwestern Americans who have never traveled outside the United States to visit a non-English-speaking country for their next vacation. Whether they are American or not, participants often start by making assumptions about the fictitious Midwesterners. "Well, we've got to sell Billy Bob on Thai food," they say, or "What's the closest thing to a dude ranch in Paris?" Participants start with what they assume they know about their audience members rather than what they know about themselves. But the dynamics of the exercise change when I ask participants to shift their emphasis from the fact that their audience is composed of people from the Midwest to the fact that those people have never traveled outside of the United States. I ask the participants to think about their own first trip to a foreign country. "What concerns or questions would you have going to a foreign country for the first time?" I ask, and the participants start to think more empathetically: How long is the flight? What currency do they use? What language is spoken? What type of food can I expect to eat? Then I ask the participants to rethink their presentation strategy.

What I'm asking the participants to do is cut through the noise to what's really important. This is what brands need to do in order to have better conversations with their audience members. Brands are conditioned to say, "Our company can do this; our product can do that." But when brand marketers fail to put themselves in their audience's shoes—when they forget to consider consumers' needs, fears, desires, and other emotional connections—they inadvertently bypass the building blocks of insights.

Exercising empathy in the pursuit of insights can be enriching personally and professionally. Without assumptions and biases blocking your way, you'll begin to see the world differently and hear people in ways you did not before. You will start to recognize new patterns, trends, and ideological intersections. In other words, you'll open yourself to insights.

CONVERSATIONS MATTER MORE NOW THAN EVER BEFORE

Conversations matter more now than ever before for one simple reason: fewer and fewer people are having them.

In the digital world, everyone is pressed for time. Businesses are no exception. With all of the relatively inexpensive technology available for tracking and predicting consumer behavior, fewer and fewer companies are embracing the idea that meaningful conversations are worthwhile investments. Yet these are precisely what consumers want.

This may seem counterintuitive, given the plethora of cheap or free options consumers currently have for communicating. Think Skype, Viber, WhatsApp, Snapchat, and the sea of social media channels to choose from. With all of this, how is it that they can still claim to be suffering from a dearth of emotionally significant connection with friends and family?

The answer is the paradox of choice. With nearly endless options and choices at their fingertips, people often fail to choose among them. This also holds true in the business world. Firms must focus on achieving their most important goals. No matter the company's product or service, productive customer communication must be one of them.

Traditionally, engaging in conversations with customers

was time- and labor-intensive. But in the digital world, this is no longer the case. As we've discussed, the various social media outlets provide no- and low-cost options for brands to collect and solicit customer feedback. What's more, insight-driven platforms, such as my own, iResearch.com, can help brands facilitate conversations faster, cheaper, and on a global scale.

Today, the critical question regarding the costs of customer conversations is this: What will it cost you *not* to have them, leaving insights buried? Remember, the marketplace will speak to you. You must decide whether you're going to listen sooner or later, and whether you're going to listen well. You must decide whether you're going to exercise empathy and curiosity, and whether you're willing to innovate away from what might not be working—and toward what could.

GETTING TO *AHA!*

Together in this book, we will make *aha!* moments come to us. We will look at the underlying dynamics of consumers' decision-making habits and the overarching sociocultural and technological trends that are influencing these today. Along the way, we will survey the modern brand landscape, including the burgeoning influence of small but highly influential industry disruptors. Above all, we will return again and again to the importance of today's insights—tomorrow's facts—and learn to leverage them for innovation and differentiation.

We stand now at the gates of chapter one, where we will discuss what brands need to know about human nature, the essence of innovation, and the product life cycles every brand faces.

CHAPTER ONE

↓

BRANDING AND HUMAN NATURE

Understanding human needs is half the job of meeting them.

ADLAI E. STEVENSON II

When businesses talk about "branding" their products or services, what they are really talking about is *humanizing* them—making them both accessible and desirable to their audiences. Doing this requires a deep understanding of the brand and its audience's aspirations. It also requires building relationships with trust and respect, inspiring brand loyalty and commitment.

Consider McDonald's, arguably one of the world's most successful brands. Go to any McDonald's anywhere in the world, and you'll find nearly identical menus. Whether you visit one in New York, London, or Shanghai, you know what to expect. You trust your experience will be consistent because McDonald's delivers this experience the same way, every time, everywhere around the world. Customers take comfort in this and reward the fast-food giant with their loyalty. Whether you're a fan of McDonald's or not, you can't deny that companies of all stripes try to build this kind of brand recognition and devotion.

How has McDonald's come to command such global attention and allegiance? By thoroughly understanding its customers and delivering what they want and need in the way they want and need it. McDonald's empathizes with its customers and tailors its offerings to suit what they actually want. In essence, McDonald's did this by gathering *insights* and structuring its business around them.

HUMAN NATURE: A PRIMER

There are certain truths of human nature that are worth considering as you pursue insights to help you humanize your brand.

WE SEE GLASSES AS EITHER HALF-FULL OR HALF-EMPTY

Each of us takes a position on a half-filled glass: we say it's half-empty or it's half-full. Neither perspective is more "right" than the other. Whatever we say, there's the same amount of wine in front of us. But those of us who say the glass is half-full also tend to be motivated to pursue pleasure, while those of us who say it's half-empty tend to be motivated to avoid fear.

Of course, every brand's audience contains individuals with each viewpoint. But which perspective is more powerful or prevalent will vary according to the product or service in question. If you're an insurance company, for example, understanding your audience's fears and how far they will go to assuage them will be critical to your efforts to humanize the various products you'll provide. On the other hand, if you're selling luxury handbags, you'll need to gain insight into just how far your potential consumers will go for the pleasure of toting your accessory around town.

WE HAVE LIMITED RESOURCES

To some extent, we all experience scarcity. None of us has more than 24 hours in a day. We spring forward and fall back here and there, trying to cheat the clock, but we never actually manage to eke out any more time from our days. We need eight hours for sleep, that fountain of youth, and another eight for work. The final eight we tend to reserve for the "good stuff" that gives our lives meaning: family, friends, fun, and food.

Time is one commodity in short supply. And for most of us, money is another. So if your product or service makes a consumer's experience cheaper, faster, or easier, then your chances of being successful dramatically increase. Achieve two or more of these, and your chances increase further still.

WE CRAVE EXPERIENCES

As we'll discuss in more detail in chapter four, we don't buy products or services as much as we buy experiences. We are motivated by the entertainment and feel-good value we believe a service or product will provide. Whether it's a consumer product or an online service, we are inclined to make purchase decisions based on how we believe a good or service will make us *feel*.

Eighty percent of brand and market decisions are primarily based on intuition.

MIT SLOAN STUDY[1]

Our inner thoughts say, "I like this because it really makes me look good, innovative, smart, and avant-garde to my friends, family, and colleagues." Our experience of a product extends far beyond its utility, earning us the

---

1   As quoted in Shruti Joshi, "Moneyball for Marketing: Why Analytics Are Critical for a Win," CMO.com, October 14, 2011, accessed June 18, 2018, at https://www.cmo.com/features/articles/2011/10/14/moneyball-for-marketing-why-analytics-are-critical-for-a-win.html#gs.MF5aVhk.

adulation of those around us. Even packaging can deliver an experience. "Just opening the box feels good," many consumers I've interviewed have told me. "The way it's carefully designed makes me feel important, like I'm a valued customer."

Exclusivity is another experience consumers tend to enjoy. For example, a good friend of mine owns a pair of high-end skis. The company that makes them deliberately limits distribution, eschewing advertising and relying wholly on word of mouth to drive sales. The skis are extremely popular among those "in the know." But this raises the question: If the skis became more mainstream, would this diminish the value of the experience of owning them to the point where current superfans of the skis stopped buying them? Without the cachet of exclusivity, would the skis be less desirable? Worth less to the people who buy them? According to my friend and other fans of the brand I interviewed, the answer is yes.

This is why it's important to understand what motivates your audience.

Here is another example from my files. A few years ago, some colleagues and I conducted a study on chocolate. Our goal was to understand the relationship people—especially women—have with it, and how this influences their purchasing habits. What we found was that women love chocolate but also feel guilty every time they eat it or even *think* about it. We also discovered, however, that the more women hear and talk about chocolate, the more likely they are to buy and/or eat it within the near future. In other words, the guilt that talk of chocolate inspired actually drove purchases. Counterintuitive, perhaps, but true.

Then, we took the study one step further: we looked into what happened after the guilt-inspired purchases had been made. Participants tended to eat just a small amount of the chocolate they'd purchased, saving the remainder or simply throwing it away.

This seemingly inconsequential behavior has reshaped the chocolate market. After discovering it, chocolatiers began selling chocolate in individually wrapped bite-size chunks and even smaller pieces. Today, even M&Ms are sold in a mini version, offering up tiny bits of chocolate and just a little bit of guilt.

WE SEEK PURPOSE

Armed with unprecedented amounts of information about the various social and environmental challenges facing the world today, consumers are increasingly saying, "I don't just want to buy a product that can help me; I want to buy a product that also benefits *the world*." More and more, they are taking companies to task for making money at the expense of the environment or underpaid laborers. With more and more providers of goods and services to choose from, consumers are leveraging their purchasing power to make decisions about the health of the planet and global labor practices. And it often costs them little or nothing to do it.

Given the choice between buying a product that delivers a good experience or buying one that delivers a good experience *and improves the world*, consumers are increasingly choosing the latter. Smart companies are recognizing this opportunity to serve several masters at once and are pushing themselves to take on the broader responsibility their audiences demand. According to Kantar Consulting's 2018 report, "Purpose 2020: Inspiring Purpose-Led Growth," brands that are perceived to have a significantly positive impact on consumers' lives have increased their value 175 percent during the last 12 years, while brands perceived to have a less positive impact have increased their value just 70 percent.[2] Brands seeking to become purpose-led organizations must home in on their philanthropic goals—not just profit and positioning but also sustainability and social purpose.

This is why I say that the successful brands of the future will be those that embody the "Triple Bottom Line" (TBL).

---

2   Kantar Consulting, "Purpose 2020: Inspiring Purpose-Led Growth," 2018, accessed May 2, 2018, at https://consulting.kantar.com/media/1286/purpose-2020_white-paper-final.pdf.

Developed by John Elkington in his 1998 book, *Cannibals with Forks: The Triple Bottom Line of 21st Century Business*, TBL is the notion that businesses should assess their performance in terms of three key aspects: profit, people, and the planet. Elkington's book inspired countless companies to evaluate their profits and losses in conjunction with appraisals of their environmental and social impacts.

Regardless of whether your organization makes such a formal commitment, it must appreciate that consumers are more informed and empowered than ever before. Their purchasing decisions are multifaceted and take companies' broader agendas and impacts into account. The same holds true for employees, who seek to serve companies that strive for revenue growth *and* positive social impact. Millennials, in particular, look beyond salary figures to questions about whether a given role is one they can feel good about. They constantly question whether their job motivates them to wake up and work every day, and whether the organization they associate with is one they are proud to be a part of.

I've seen this shift among the undergraduate and MBA students I teach in the United States and abroad. Not long ago, I conducted an informal poll, asking students whether they intended to pursue a career within an organization or start their own business. Ninety percent indicated the latter. This represents a major shift from the 1990s and early 2000s, when the vast majority of students planned to pursue jobs in finance, law, or medicine. But what's even more interesting is that all of these fledgling entrepreneurs were very clear that their future businesses would execute on two fronts: profitability and social impact. Emboldened by the successes of other entrepreneurs and the relatively low financial and logistical barriers to entry, many of my former students have gone live with their ideas, launching digital publicity campaigns to get themselves and their ventures noticed.

CASE STUDY: WARBY PARKER

Founded by four students at the Wharton School at the University of Pennsylvania, Warby Parker is an online and brick-and-mortar retailer of eyeglasses. According to its website, "Warby Parker was founded with a rebellious spirit and a lofty objective: to offer designer eyewear at a revolutionary price, while leading the way for socially conscious businesses."

Upon discovering that the eyewear industry had long been dominated by a single player who had been able to keep prices artificially high, Warby Parker's founders strove to provide "higher-quality, better-looking prescription eyewear at a fraction of the going price" by "circumventing traditional channels, designing glasses in-house, and engaging with customers directly." They also committed to creating social good: "We believe everyone has the right to see," reads the company site. Sure enough, Warby Parker partners with distributors around the globe to donate one pair of glasses to someone in need for each pair it sells.[3]

Named for two characters featured in a journal by author Jack Kerouac, Warby Parker was founded in 2010 with a $2,500 grant from Wharton's Venture Initiation Program. As of March 2018, the private company was valued at $1.75 billion.[4]

Despite its increase in visibility, the search for purpose in business transactions is not new. It's a natural desire among humans who depend on one another and the planet for their survival and prosperity. The difference in the digital age is the ease and speed with which the majority of the world's population can access information. Anything

---

3 "History," Warby Parker website, accessed June 1, 2017, at https://www.warbyparker.com/history.

4 Jason Del Rey, "Warby Parker Is Valued at $1.75 Billion after a Pre-IPO Investment of $75 Million," Recode.com, accessed June 15, 2018, at https://www.recode.net/2018/3/14/17115230/warby-parker-75-million-funding-t-rowe-price-ipo.

someone might want to know is quite literally at their fingertips 24 hours per day.

CASE STUDY: PEDIGREE DOG FOOD

In 2007, Pedigree launched a campaign that not only boosted its brand and profits but also transformed the company. This initiative put the pet food brand's purpose of helping dogs help the world right at the center of its marketing and innovation strategies.

Pedigree's "Dogs Rule" campaign began with an ad showing dogs locked in cages narrated by David Duchovny. Within it, Pedigree promised that if customers bought Pedigree dog food, the company would make a donation to help shelter dogs find loving homes. The ad aired during the two-day Westminster Kennel Club Dog Show, during which the company collected more than $500,000 in pledges.

Since that time, Pedigree's campaign has become the cornerstone of the brand's image. From the United States to New Zealand to France, Pedigree has become known as a company devoted to dogs' wellness. Although many dog owners have traditionally based their dog food purchasing decisions on price, the campaign has given them something bigger to participate in.

As Chris Mondzelewski, vice president of marketing for Pedigree's parent company, Mars Petcare U.S., put it, "We have a fundamental belief that dogs do an enormous amount of good for society. We have studies that show this statistically, so if we do good for dogs, obviously through the food we're providing, but also through the shelter work, [then] it will resonate with our consumers. If they see us doing that, we become a brand with a mission they want to buy into as well."[5]

---

5   Jeff Beer, "How Pedigree Turned Doing Good for Dogs into Good Marketing for Dog Food," *Fast Company*, May 28, 2015, accessed June 1, 2017, at https://www.fastcompany.com/3046691/how-pedigree-turned-doing-good-for-dogs-into-good-marketing-for-dog-food.

Sure enough, Pedigree's customers have bought into it. The company's move from direct product messaging toward socially conscious advertising has boosted its advertising effectiveness by 40 percent. Although the pet care company has experimented with product- and ingredient-focused ads, it has realized that "playing at that higher emotional level with consumers, really helping them understand what dogs can do for them and that we share that belief, has really resonated when we look at what's been most successful for the brand."[6]

Pedigree continues to deploy socially conscious branding around the globe, most notably with its "Feed the Good" campaign. Launched in 2015, the campaign advocates for adopting dogs from shelters and generates awareness around the good that dogs provide human beings and society.[7] Alongside the campaign, Pedigree works to live out its message. "We're not going to go out and create campaigns about shelters and dogs doing good unless we're doing all these things behind the scenes to make sure dogs are finding loving homes," Mondzelewski explains. "In today's day and age, consumers will see through you and know if you're really all about the values you claim."[8]

PUTTING THE PIECES TOGETHER

Ultimately, humanizing a brand requires you to understand and play up its human elements. Whether you're looking to connect with an external audience or with your employees, you need to understand what's driving their perceptions, emotions, and decision making. If you do so successfully, you'll cultivate conversations that help you grasp the needs, fears, desires, and other emotional

---

6   Ibid.

7   Ibid.

8   Ibid.

connections—the *why*—underlying their behaviors. Why do people choose A over B? Why do they say C? Why do they think D? Answering these questions will help you get to the *aha!* moments that can guide your delivery of products, services, and *experiences* that resonate and inspire loyalty.

THE ROLE OF CONTROL: BRANDS

All brands worry about control: controlling their market share, their consumers, their messaging, their bottom line. But the reality is, none of us—brands or individual human beings—have as much control as we'd like to think.

I know from personal experience that I control almost nothing—not other people, not the weather, not the world's events. All I can control is myself, and even this I can do only about half the time. As much as I try to remain focused, my own thoughts and emotions are constantly trying to distract me. It's taken me years to learn that the more I try to exert control over others, the less control I end up with.

Surely, you might think, brands have more control than individuals do. But as you'll see, that is seldom the case.

KEEP YOUR FOCUS ON YOURSELF

When it comes to control, brands can be a lot like people:

they want to have control over everything—their market, their competitors, and their customers. But the truth is, they're limited as well. The most important lesson a business leader can learn is to remain focused on what the company does best, why it does so, and how it can improve.

Business leaders' desire for control often manifests itself in keeping too close an eye on what their competitors are doing. While there is value for a company in being aware of key industry peers' products, services, and messaging, there is also serious danger in becoming *too* concerned about these. Companies can waste precious resources trying to emulate the competitors they perceive as threats when those resources would be better spent on creating superior versions of *themselves*. As the adage goes, "Be yourself, because everyone else is taken."

In short, if you want to differentiate yourself from your competition, you need to be a leader, not a follower. Stop wasting your time worrying about what other companies are doing. Don't wonder whether you can control or emulate them, because you cannot. Keep your focus on yourself and what you do best, and strive to do it better and better.

By this I mean, become your *own competitor*. Strive to out-innovate *yourself*. Get closer to your audience. Learn more about their pain points and problems. Understand the larger forces at work in their decision making. See opportunities where you and your competitors have all failed to deliver the solutions you are seeking. Then leverage your insights to innovate, differentiate, and inspire a loyal, long-term following.

DEFINE YOUR SANDBOX

How you define your sandbox determines how far your brand can go and how big it can become. If your sandbox is filled with your direct competitors, then being the "best" among them will be your ultimate goal. But if you look beyond your peers—out at the possibility of being the best product or service in your category *in the world*—this changes both your perspective *and* your possibilities for innovation and success. The world of higher education provides an illustrative example of a limiting sandbox. Rankings published by outlets such as *U.S. News & World Report* and *Princeton Review* are considered critical determinants of the value of a school's brand. Institutions often try to ascend in the rankings by improving on the factors that the publishing reviewers use rather than on their academic offerings and infrastructure that might *actually* make their school better for students and faculty. When they concentrate on such banalities, schools often miss opportunities to capitalize on what makes their institutions unique and desirable, including extra-campus factors such as their geographic location and alumni, employer, and academic partner networks. Spending resources "teaching to the test" rather than on true leadership and differentiation can harm schools not just in these rankings but also in the long term. Misguided initiatives can take years to undo.

Universities trying to work their way into the top 25 or 50 schools on a given publication's list also seem to forget that in order for them to advance up the ladder, other schools need to fall down a few rungs. Higher-ranking schools understand that in order to maintain their status, they need to constantly innovate. This means that lower-ranking schools that endeavor to emulate them end up in a constant chase, modeling themselves on yesterday's differentiators.

My advice to any brand seeking to innovate is this: Return to your roots. To become a leader, reconnect with who you are, what you do best, and what you uniquely "own." Know your strengths—your core differentiators—and have conversations with your audience about what they think, feel, and want. Dig into their perceptions of you, your products and services, and your competitors; always remember that their perception is reality. Learn how to connect and reconnect with your audience to foster the sort of long-term relationships that drive sustained profitability. Then let your competition chase *you*. They'll have a tough time replicating your efforts.

Becoming their own best competitor and constantly innovating is important for established companies as well. Even they don't have the control they might imagine they do. The story of consumer-products giant Gillette and upstart Dollar Shave Club is the perfect reminder for brands that might get a big head.

In 2012, Gillette (owned by Procter & Gamble since 2005) dominated the US razor market, claiming a share of 72 percent. For years, the company's strategy had been to do more of what had made it a success: Gillette periodically increased the number of blades on its razors and added features such as vibrating handles, moisturizing strips, and flashlights. With every iteration, Gillette made its razors more expensive. They became so expensive, in fact, that stores had to keep them in locked plexiglass boxes, requiring purchasers to seek out store clerks to access the razors.

Then, 34-year-old Michael Dubin entered the men's shaving scene. Dubin was frustrated by the cumbersome and costly razor-buying process that involved finding a clerk to unlock the "razor fortress" for the privilege of paying too much for too few razors. He was also convinced that if he could mail blades to customers for less than they'd pay in the store, they'd sign on for a subscription service. When a family friend asked Dubin if he was willing to unload a warehouse full of surplus blades, Dubin accepted the challenge. In March 2012, he launched Dollar Shave Club with a $4,500 YouTube video.[9] In it, Dubin proclaimed his company's blades were "f***ing great," and the video went viral. Dubin received 12,000 orders that day.[10]

From there, Dollar Shave Club took off. Again and again, the company improved its products and services to fulfill its consumers' needs better and better. These iterations included releasing a full range of men's grooming products and providing relevant education and guidance at no cost. By 2015, the company's sales had risen to $263 million. Competitors such as Harry's and ShaveMOB popped up, and Amazon launched a service of its own. So did Gillette. The "Gillette Shave Club" resorted to tweeting claims such as "two million guys and counting no longer buy from the other shave clubs."[11] But in 2016, Dollar Shave Club claimed 51 percent of the online market, while Gillette controlled just over 21 percent of it.

When Unilever purchased it for $1 billion in 2016, the privately held Dollar Shave Club was on track to generate $250 million in annual revenues.[12] By that time, Gillette's

---

9   See Dollar Shave Club, "Our Blades Are F***ing Great," YouTube.com, https://youtu.be/ZUG9qYTJMsI.

10   Jaclyn Trop, "How Dollar Shave Club's Founder Built a $1 Billion Company That Changed the Industry," *Entrepreneur*, March 28, 2017, accessed June 1, 2017, at https://www.entrepreneur.com/article/290539.

11   Ibid.

12   Ibid.

total market share had fallen from a high of 72 percent to just 54 percent.[13] In June 2017, the *Wall Street Journal* announced that Gillette would be slashing prices of its razors by as much as 20 percent.[14]

The lesson for brands is this: Even with 72 percent market share, you can't control your customers. Furthermore, you can't control the frustrated users of your products who can enter your space and disrupt it with very little backing. It's critical to remember that the more market share you claim, the more tempted you'll be to exert control—a losing battle in the long run.

As a brand, the best you can do is become your own best competitor. Look for ways to out-innovate yourself. Accept that leading requires constantly innovating, even when doing so might render your own products and services obsolete.

CONSUMERS AND CONTROL

Consumers like choice because it gives them a sense of control. Choices are empowering. But here's the rub: too many choices can be paralyzing, ruining a consumer's

---

13   Brad Tuttle, "Gillette Is Finally Slashing Its Razor Prices," *Money*, April 4, 2017, accessed June 1, 2017, at http://time.com/money/4724823/gillette-razor-prices-cut/.

14   Sharon Terlep, "Gillette, Bleeding Market Share, Cuts Prices of Razors," *Wall Street Journal*, April 4, 2017, accessed June 1, 2017, at https://www.wsj.com/articles/gillette-bleeding-market-share-cuts-prices-of-razors-1491303601.

experience. Even the audience-savvy Dollar Shave Club ran into this problem, adding so many items to its suite of men's grooming products that its members became overwhelmed by choice and sought a more limited selection instead.

Sometimes, a plethora of choices of products, services, or features can arise out of a disconnect between a company's marketers and engineers. Engineers are trained to solve problems. For them, the more solutions, the better. But marketers, who tend to be more tightly in tune with human nature, know this can lead to problems on the user side.

I ran into this when I was developing my insight platform, iResearch.com. I worked closely with a software engineer who was determined to maximize its functionality. We were discussing what data-sorting options to give users, and the engineer was thrilled to tell me he'd come up with *twelve* options. "Look," he said, revealing a drop-down menu with all twelve options listed, some of which I didn't quite understand myself. "The user can sort the data almost any way they want."

"But what about any way they *need*?" I asked him. "How did you end up with the twelve options?" "Because I could," he said.

That is the difference between marketers and engineers.

Marketers are market-driven; engineers are product-driven. Some companies—often those led by former engineers—lose sight of the customer's experience in their quest to create the perfect mousetrap. These businesses can lose track of the impetus that drove the development of the better mousetrap in the first place. This is why brands always need to temper their quest to bring new products and services to the marketplace with an awareness of what consumers are willing to pay, what kinds of experiences their products and services create, and how many choices serve their customers' need for control without paralyzing them.

Successful brands take all perspectives into account: the engineers', the marketers', the consumers', the investors' or shareholders'. They understand the motivations and limitations of each, welcoming each group's feedback at every stage of the development process. They have not just market instincts but also audience members' insights that help them confidently act on those instincts.

THE IMPACT OF LIMITING CHOICE

When it comes time to decide the ideal number of choices of products or services to offer your consumers, strive for simplicity.

Apple does this extremely well. The tech titan has deliberately limited the number of iPhone, iPad, and iMac options available. In general, it offers three options for memory, size, and color—not twelve, not fifteen; three.

Apple does the same in its application environment. The company exerts extreme control over its App Store, limiting developers' access to it and, therefore, consumers' options. App purchasers looking for a more open environment have an option: the Android platform. But with this comes other problems, including the increased chance of a device being exposed to damaging malware. Apple made the decision to help users avoid these issues, deliberately limiting users' choices while preserving the integrity, safety, predictability, and simplicity of the Apple experience.

Companies in other industries have begun to follow Apple's example of limiting choice to streamline the consumer experience. For example, during the last two decades, auto makers have radically simplified the buying process by streamlining different models' options packages. What these and other industry leaders have discovered is that too many choices lead to buyers' indecision. This can compromise buyers' engagement with products and, in some cases, prevent them from making purchases at all.

Again, keep in mind that your audience is pressed for time.

They want choice, yes. But they don't want to waste time sifting through countless alternatives. Whatever industry you're in, your goal should be to generate engagement with your product or service, not to discourage it by confusing or complicating your audience's experience.

At the end of the day, consumers want choices—but not limitless choices. They don't want to waste precious time, and they don't want to be confused. They want to know what they can expect from brands, and they want any experiences associated with them to be predictable and uncomplicated.

THE POWER OF THREE—AND TWO

Throughout human history, the power of three has stood firm. Whether it's found in a religious trilogy or a play in three acts, the natural rhythm of three is suited to our human capacity to understand, process, and remember. Think about it: no allegorical genie says he'll grant you *four* wishes.

When we think about contemporary companies that leverage the power of three to great effect, we think of Nike. *Just Do It*, the brand tells us.

"Just do it" is rhythmic, simple, and versatile. The phrase can mean different things to different people at different times. But in every instance, it conveys urgency in a direct and unmistakable way, tapping into our tendency to respond positively to information conveyed in three parts. Those three words also convey Nike's message of empowerment through will and action. The implicit directive is this: Don't think about it; *just do it*. Don't anguish about whether you should start walking, running, or working out in some other way; *just do it*, and you'll be happy you did.

The inverted pyramid on top represents Nike's brand essence: *Just Do It*. The bottom pyramid represents the dissemination of this message to Nike's vast audience.

Think about your own brand. How can you distill everything you are—your spirit, purpose, and aspirations—into three concise, powerful, and versatile words? Make the message as simple, direct, and impactful as possible, and consider the external experience it inspires for your customers. What emotions does it stir up? What images does it conjure? All of this determines how your audience will be touched, motivated, and inspired by your message. The trio's emotional brunt also dictates whether the message will take hold in a way that drives your audience's interest and loyalty the way *Just Do It* supports Nike's.

Believe it or not, a two-word message can be even more powerful than a series of three. To be sure, it's harder to distill your core purpose and message into two words than three. But if you can, your message is likely to stick.

Consider Apple's *Think Different*. Like *Just Do It*, the directive to *Think Different* showcases what Apple's brand is about and what Apple does. From product design to retailing to packaging, Apple has been thinking and doing differently since its founding.

PRICING: AN ADDITIONAL OPPORTUNITY TO INTRODUCE SIMPLICITY INTO THE CUSTOMER EXPERIENCE

For brands that are looking to streamline their customer experience, pricing provides opportunities for innovation.

Too often, brands don't adequately simplify their pricing. This creates too many opportunities for bean counting, which quickly becomes a pebble in the consumer's shoe—a source of constant irritation that drives them nuts and detracts from their experience. As more and more companies come to understand this, industry leaders are taking steps to simplify their pricing.

The car industry offers up an example. For decades, the purchase price of cars varied widely according to the selected options and the negotiations that happened at dealerships. This made it difficult for consumers to predict—and control—the prices of the vehicles they purchased, and it gave salespeople bad reputations. Now, Volvo offers greater flexibility with subscription pricing that covers everything for a fixed monthly fee on its XC40 compact SUV.[15]

Another example comes from the mobile phone industry. For decades, wireless carriers have been notorious for nickeling-and-diming customers, forcing them to dissect charges for minutes and data. Now, providers such as T-Mobile are taking steps to simplify their plans, making monthly costs more predictable for customers and the process of selecting a plan less complex.

THE NEW BRAND LANDSCAPE

More and more frequently, today's entrepreneurs are saying, "I don't care what the world says; I think I can create X or do Y in a new way that will better serve an

---

15   Roberto Baldwin, "Add a Luxury Volvo to Your List of Monthly Subscriptions," March 2, 2018, Engadget.com, accessed April 29, 2018, at https://www.engadget.com/2018/03/02/volvo-xc40-care-by-volvo-hands-on/.

audience I know is out there." Platforms including Kickstarter are providing a way for innovators to get to proof of concept without securing lots of investment first.

Too often, would-be entrepreneurs seek out investment too soon. The reality is, very few startups are backed by angel investors or venture capitalists. According to data compiled by *Entrepreneur*, fewer than 1 percent receive such funding. In fact, 57 percent of startups are started with personal funds or credit, and roughly 40 percent are backed by friends and family.[16]

If you are truly inspired by a particular issue or problem and think you've got a great solution on your hands, bring your idea to the marketplace cheaply and easily by having conversations first. Start talking to your potential customers on Kickstarter, Facebook, Twitter, or any number of other channels that are free or inexpensive to use. Then turn your idea into a prototype using their feedback. Once you hit this stage, having incorporated data from conversations and gained traction with your audience along the way, you'll be ready to discuss equity partnerships with potential investors.

In this way, conversations can have a tremendous impact on your initial survivability and your ultimate success. *Have them.* Don't be the expert. Resist the urge to persuade your audience of the greatness of your idea. Instead,

---

16   Laura Entis, "Where Startup Funding Really Comes From," *Entrepreneur*, November 20, 2013, accessed May 29, 2018, at https://www.entrepreneur.com/article/230011.

sit back and listen to what they have to say about it. As much as you need to be passionate and enthusiastic about your product or service, you must leave your emotions at the door during these conversations. It's not important what *you* think about your product; it's important how *others* feel, think, and respond to what you bring to the table. Seek to understand their needs and desires—and, of course, what they are willing to pay to fulfill them.

Conversations can also help you determine how best to differentiate your product or service in the marketplace. For example, you may find out that although your offering is not unique, your pricing or placement makes it more accessible and appealing to consumers. Even the user experience your website or app provides could be your differentiator. Dollar Shave Club didn't reinvent men's razors after all; it made the purchasing experience cheaper, faster, easier, and more fun. Apple didn't invent the MP3 player either, but it did give consumers an affordable, cool way to carry music in their pockets.

Engage with your audience as early as possible to determine how to differentiate your product or service. There are many ways to do this, and conversations can help you figure it out.

BRINGING PRODUCTS TO MARKET: ENGINEERS VS. MARKETERS

As we discussed earlier, engineers are product-driven, while marketers are market-driven. You need both perspectives for a successful product launch, and each can be augmented by what your audience has to tell you.

Recently, I participated in a hardware-oriented hackathon in Ireland. I was part of a group that was tasked with coming up with a new product idea that my teammates and I could market to the other conference attendees. Eight of us were engineers; two were marketers. Our idea was for a new kind of badge for people to wear at conferences.

Rather than a traditional paper name tag encased in plastic, our badge was electronic. To make introductions more engaging and expedient, it featured image and video capability. It also incorporated a tracking mechanism that could help people connect. We wanted to facilitate the sort of serendipity conference attendees seek, so we designed our badges to do this.

In discussing the badge's features and capabilities, we became increasingly persuaded of its genius. But then I interrupted, "Why do we need to come up with a whole new device? Why can't we make this a phone-based app?" After all, if we created an entirely new device, we would be competing screen- and hardware-wise with something people were already carrying in their pocket. Adding to this was the cost of the unit, which we estimated at $70. Would conference organizers be willing or able to add this to attendees' costs? Then there was the matter of breakage and loss of these small devices.

Thinking like a marketer rather than an engineer, I said, "Let's focus on creating an app to facilitate serendipity instead of creating an entirely new device." Perhaps all we needed, I suggested, was a radio-frequency identification (RFID) tag to attach to attendees' existing badges. I pointed out that an RFID solution could help avoid device competition and cost cents instead of dollars to implement. But the engineers resisted the idea of creating an app because it did not entail creating a new device.

I lost that battle. Then my group lost the war. In the end, we could not get the prototype to work. The hackathon judges also took us to task on all the points I'd raised: cost, risk of breakage, and addition of an unnecessary device. The engineers in our group had come up with a potential solution to the problem, but the concept's user experience simply wasn't viable. Like the software engineer who'd helped build out my insights platform and wanted to give users twelve ways to sort their data because he *could*, these hackathon engineers had hoped to put their training to use. But in the end, they hadn't come up with a solution that could work in the marketplace. The moral of the story is that both engineers and marketers are critical to product development and launch. Whether you're an entrepreneur who is playing both roles or working in a group of which both are members, it's important to remember that you need both perspectives to come up with a solution that is functional, practical, and priced appropriately. Most importantly, you must make the user experience shine.

ALWAYS KEEP YOUR OBJECTIVE IN MIND

A magician, a priest, and an engineer are going to be executed by guillotine. Each is given a choice: faceup or facedown.

The magician goes first. He chooses to be facedown in the guillotine. The executioner pulls the string that drops the blade, but nothing happens. Onlookers marvel. "Wow!" they say. "He really is a magician! He stopped the blade!" The magician is free to go.

The priest goes next. "I'm a man of God," he says and chooses to face upward at the heavenly skies. Again, the executioner pulls on the string, and again, the blade does not fall. The crowd is amazed. "God saved him!" they cry out. "He must truly be a man of God!" The priest is free to go.

The engineer is the last in the guillotine. He chooses to face upward as the priest did. Just as the executioner reaches for the string, the engineer says, "Ah! I see your problem! The pin up there is holding the blade in place."

Moral of the story: Always keep your objective in mind.

THE LIFE CYCLES OF BRANDS

Every product has a life cycle. When an innovation is first introduced into the marketplace, competitors see an opportunity and flock to it. They create new, enhanced versions without altering the innovation's core, growing its market-wide customer base. In time, however, the product's novelty wears off. Then the innovators who had seen a chance to capitalize on differentiation sense that the market has become saturated, and they move on to the next opportunity. Once this entrepreneurial energy dwindles away, a product or service enters a phase of maturity. Ultimately, it declines.

The world of fashion offers some perspective into products' life cycles. Follow fashion trends, and you'll see that styles need about one generation to move through the stages of innovation, growth, maturity, and decline before they resurface and kick off the cycle again. Consider big sunglasses, for example. Walk down any city street these days, and you'll see how "in" they are. But if you've been walking down city streets for at least 20 years, you'll know they've simply come around again. Men's ties are another example. They become wider, narrower, and wider again as women's dresses become longer and shorter and longer and shorter. It's all about the cycle of innovation, growth, maturity, and decline. The last phase clears the way for reinvigorated interest and reinvention, and for the life cycle to begin again.

Brands that recognize these cycles can use them to build strategies for remaining relevant to their fan base over the long term. Companies can struggle to remain realistic and prepare for the eventual fall when their product is sitting atop hype mountain. But it's critical to prepare for the inevitable. Similarly, brands can struggle with the downside when their product or service is entering the phase of declining popularity. Eventually, these brands would do well to remember that an upswing will take hold. Brands that stick around for the long haul position themselves to seize on the cycle's opportunities and weather its busts.

In order to maintain this "bigger picture" perspective, remember that it's all about balance. If you're Gillette, for example, and things are going well—perhaps *too* well—it's important to recognize that extremes are unsustainable. Sooner or later, something you can neither predict nor control is bound to bring you back into line. The push and pull of balance always prevails. There is no explaining this phenomenon. It's simply an aspect of the beauty and joy of the universe that it strives for balance in every instance. Accept this, and prepare to take action as the pendulum starts to swing.

Don't be surprised by the unavoidable, and don't let the extremes of success or struggle engulf you. Resist the temptation to focus on market share and stock price, or to use these metrics as indicators that your control of the market is locked in. Recognize that you're in a vulnerable position, not a powerful one; that challengers, naysayers, and disruptors are about to encroach into your space. Listen when they tell you, "It can't be the case that consumers are going to be willing to pay more and more for razors that can function only marginally better, if at all. It can't be that people are going to continue to waste time in stores asking for assistance unlocking plexiglass containers. There has to be a better way. And someone is going to find it. Let that someone be us."

Remember also that *remaining* in balance is a constant challenge. Just as the universe strives for it, so should you. You can't predict the future, but you can recognize when you are out of balance. When you start swinging in one direction, take notice and avoid going too far. Know you're vulnerable when you hit a peak, and trust that opportunities to harness the energy of a new cycle can abound when you're in a valley. Keep striving to come up with ways to deliver better experiences for your audience, competing with your existing ways of doing things. Remember that your competitors are always waiting in the wings, armed with affordable tools and ways to disrupt even the biggest industries and the most entrenched players.

As you take these steps, keep conversations at the fore: conversations with your customers, your employees, and even other industry leaders. Seek out advocates for consumers who will play the role of devil's advocate for you. Find people who will tell you that more blades and higher prices are not "innovations" that produce a better experience. Input from contrarian voices can be more valuable than any other feedback, especially when it forces you to see things from new perspectives and breaks logjams that hinder progress. Contrarians can provide exactly the sorts of insights needed to innovate, differentiate, and form deep, sustainable connections with customers.

CHAPTER ONE TAKEAWAYS

- Humanize your product or service to brand it effectively.
- Provide standout experiences and sociocultural support to win over today's consumers.
- Leverage your audience's perceptions, emotions, and decision making to differentiate your brand and your product.
- Define your sandbox broadly and ambitiously.
- Focus on the things you can control: yourself, your company, and your product.
- Tap into the power of three—or, if you can, the power of two.

CHAPTER TWO

INSIGHTS

In today's complex and fast-moving world, what we need even more than foresight or hindsight is insight.

ISABELLE IOANNIDES

Since 1800, when the Industrial Revolution hit its stride, interest in the word *insight* has grown fivefold.

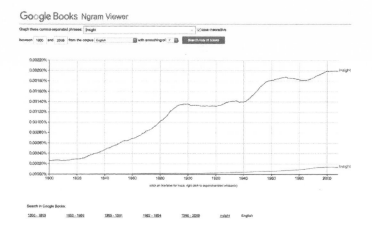

Why might the rise of industry correlate with increasing interest in insights? Well, in business, the key to success is differentiation. And insights into your market, your consumers, and the prevailing trends that drive the behavior of each are the keys to differentiation.

Although everyone is seeking insights, few agree as to what they actually *are*.

WHAT ARE INSIGHTS ANYWAY?

Let's start by defining *insight*. Oxford Living Dictionary notes that the term originally appeared in Middle English, defined as "inner sight, mental vision, wisdom," and offers the following modern interpretation:

in·sight ('in͵sīt/)
an accurate and deep understanding

But what counts as a "deep intuitive understanding" in the context of modern brands? Here, it's helpful to understand what an insight *is not*. An insight is not a single datum, nor is it a one-dimensional observation or expression of a want or a need. Rather, an insight is a combination of data, observations, and broader knowledge of macro- and microlevel technological, economic, and cultural influences on markets and consumers' desires, expectations, and decision making. Insights are rarely about the "what"; they are almost always about the "why."

Garnering insights takes time. It requires you to go outside your comfort zone in order to discover what you don't know you don't know. It requires you to remain curious and open to whatever you might discover along the way, including what concepts challenge or even contradict your assumptions or prevailing theories. This can be a lot of work, but it can also be incredibly rewarding. In fact, the insights you gather and leverage can determine whether your brand stagnates or succeeds.

What's the first step toward *getting to aha!*? Deploying what I call the Three Ingredients of Insight.

THE THREE INGREDIENTS OF INSIGHT
EMPATHY

The first ingredient of insight is empathy—the ability to step outside yourself and understand the experience of your audience. Empathy helps you craft questions that drive engaging conversations, enabling you to dig into *why*. Adopting the perspective of your audience members, whose problems your product or service aims to solve, means seeing their problems as they do and appreciating whether and how well your solution may work for them.

Empathizing requires you to be open to feedback that may run counter to what you'd anticipated or sought. But it can also help you arrive at more meaningful insights faster. The more you practice empathizing, the more natural this becomes.

CURIOSITY

A piece of information is a trailhead, while an insight is a destination. We may want to stop somewhere along the trail, assuming we've gone far enough. We may be tempted to think, "I know what I need!" and ignore the data and knowledge we've garnered from experience, observations, and conversations that challenge or contradict a finding to which we've become attached. We naturally seek out information that reinforces what we want to believe is true. Who doesn't like hearing, "You're right!"?

This is why you need heroic curiosity to chase insights. Every time you think you've compiled sufficient data, observations, and feedback—every time you believe you've dug deeply enough—say, "You know what? I might be wrong." To walk the path toward insight, you must make room for both your validating angel and your challenging devil. As with the ingredient of empathy, the more you use your curiosity, the easier and the more valuable it will become.

VISION

Once you've harnessed your empathy and curiosity to collect feedback, you'll be ready to bring your vision into play. This is your opportunity to bring your industry knowledge and experience to bear on the challenge in front of you. Your vision should be predicated on an understanding of prior innovations in your space as well as relevant past and current economic, technological, and cultural trends. Now you're ready to map out, create, and deliver a solution that not only meets your audience's expectations but also exceeds them.

Of course, as Steve Jobs said, "It's always easy to connect the dots going backwards." The real challenge we all face is connecting the dots moving forward. Doing this requires deep dedication and insight. It requires using empathy, curiosity, and vision to innovate and deliver a singular experience that strikes an emotional chord, inspiring loyalty among your external and internal audiences.

THE FACTS ARE OUTSIDE THE BUILDING

Stanford professor, author, and Silicon Valley consultant Steve Blank has famously taught that "the facts are outside the building." Blank encourages executives and entrepreneurs alike to get out of their boardrooms and seek out the raw materials for insights that lie beyond their buildings' walls. Innovation—creating new products, services, or modes of operation—requires creators to abandon their old modes of thinking and attachments to products, services, and methods.

Getting out of the building is the first step. The second is understanding the motivation of the insight seeker.

There are two types of insight seekers. The first are those who *reactively* chase insights. Feeling pressure from industry disruptors, this group operates defensively, seeking out insights that can help them defend the status quo. These insight seekers feel like they're on a speeding treadmill. Instead of picking up their own pace, they want to slow down others.

The second are insight seekers who *actively* chase insights. This group plays offense, not defense. They are unconcerned with preserving the status quo or protecting their current interests. Rather, they are bent on solving vexing problems. For these entrepreneurial individuals, conventional approaches are irrelevant. To them, the sky is, quite literally, the limit. They want to change the world, and they don't care about the rules. Patagonia founder Yvon Chouinard even likens these insight hunters to troublesome children: "If you want to understand the entrepreneur, study the juvenile delinquent," Chouinard argues. "The delinquent is saying with his actions, 'This sucks, I'm going to do my own thing.'"[17]

In the remainder of this chapter, we will consider some major corporations and startups that have collected and applied market insights. As we'll see, many have done so—some more effectively than others.

INSIGHTS AT WORK
STARBUCKS

In 2007, Starbucks was the largest specialty coffee retailer in the world. And the company was in crisis.

Since going public in 1992, Starbucks had boomed, opening hundreds of new stores around the globe each year. The company's valuation had skyrocketed along with its rapid expansion. But below the surface, all was not well.

Starbucks's expansion had eroded its customer experience. In 2007, same-store sales were declining for the first time in the company's history. As then-chairman of the board Howard Schultz explained in a company-wide memo, "Over the past ten years, in order to achieve the growth, development, and scale necessary to go from less than 1,000 stores to 13,000 stores and beyond, we have had

---

17 Scott Maxwell, "Why the AI Brain Drain Won't Last," *Inc.*, April 24, 2017, accessed June 18, 2018, at https://www.inc.com/scott-maxwell/why-the-ai-brain-drain-wont-last.html.

to make a series of decisions that, in retrospect, have led to the watering down of the Starbucks Experience, and, what some might call the commoditization of our brand."[18]

Not long after writing this memo, Schultz fired Jim Donald, the company's CEO, and returned as CEO. Schultz's goal was to reignite consumers' emotional connection to the Starbucks brand. The insight that drove his subsequent decisions was that Starbucks customers sought out a particular kind of experience in its stores—one rooted not only in the coffee but also in interactions with baristas and with one another. As Schultz explained:

> Ideally, every Starbucks store should tell a story about coffee and what we as an organization believe in. That story should unfold via the taste and presentation of our products, as well as the sights, sounds and smells that surround our customers... Our stores and partners are at their best when they collaborate to provide an oasis, an uplifting feeling of comfort, connection, as well as a deep respect for the coffee and communities we serve.[19]

Schultz understood that in order to protect Starbucks's long-term viability, every store had to deliver the *experience* its customers were looking for. Starbucks's turnaround

---

18   Howard Schultz as quoted in Nancy Koehn, "Starbucks Coffee Company: Transformation and Renewal," Harvard Business School Case Study 9-314-068, June 2014, p. 1.

19   Ibid., p. 26.

extended beyond its coffee offerings to intense training of employees across the organization. This training educated employees not only on the Starbucks in-store experience but also on the organization's larger sociocultural mission and values.

In a daring and expensive move, Schultz closed more than 7,000 Starbucks stores for espresso training. He asked store managers to post signs on the doors letting customers know that the company was reenergizing its partners and reengaging them in the Starbucks experience. Schultz also ordered that all stores replace any machinery that blocked baristas' view of customers and redesign their interiors to accommodate customers' longer stays in stores. In addition to these store-oriented innovations, Schultz brought the company's largest missions to the fore, including sponsoring a multiday training in New Orleans shortly after Hurricane Katrina. There, thousands of Starbucks partners took to the streets to assist with cleanup efforts across the city.

Schultz's efforts paid off. Within two years, Starbucks was back on track. Boosted by additional initiatives that grew out of internal brainstorming and ideas from customers via the company's new interactive website, MyStarbucksIdea.com, the company restored its financial health. As Schultz wrote in the company's August 2009 annual report, "I'm pleased to report that we have made and continue to make significant progress in transforming Starbucks and returning the company to sustainable, profitable growth."[20] After hitting a 52-week low of $14.95 in July 2008, Starbucks's share price topped $57.00 in May 2018.

KATE SPADE

While Starbucks leveraged insights to drive a massive company turnaround, the late entrepreneur Kate Spade used them to bring a new product to market—and carve out a $2.4 billion niche in the process.

As a magazine editor for *Mademoiselle* during the early 1990s, Kate Spade was immersed in the world of women's wardrobes and accessories. She saw an opportunity to develop a new kind of handbag—one that was fashionable *and* functional—and with the help of her husband and business partner, Andy Spade, she took it.

Kate Spade understood women's pain points, both as an observer of women's fashion and a consumer of it herself. She knew what frustrated fashion-conscious women. She also knew what her core audience would pay for the pairing of fashion and functionality they craved. In 1993, Spade launched a line of burlap handbags she had created.

20 Ibid.

Spade's bags were spacious and sleek. Utilitarian shapes featuring bold pops of color made them singularly appealing to modern New Yorkers, who flocked to her eponymous Manhattan retail outlet. Business boomed. Spade went on to open additional outlets in and around New York. She placed her bags on the shelves of high-end department stores, including Bloomingdale's, Saks Fifth Avenue, and Neiman Marcus. In 1999, she sold the business to Neiman Marcus, but she maintained her role in its evolution. The brand soon expanded into women's and children's clothing and housewares, and in March 2017, Coach bought the company for $2.4 billion.

When she started, Spade had no idea where she was going. She didn't know that billions of dollars could be made by building a more modern handbag—at least not until she began to trust her own insights.

SPANX

Like Kate Spade, Spanx founder Sara Blakely built one of the most popular brands in women's fashion atop her insights as an observer and a consumer. Because she did, Blakely is now America's youngest female self-made billionaire.

In 1998, Blakely was a 27-year-old fax machine saleswoman who was tired of being disappointed by how she looked in dresses that looked great on hangers. She wondered if she could extend the smoothness created by her pantyhose all the way up her torso. To her, this seemed simple enough, so she created a prototype. And it worked. Blakely was amazed at how the garment changed the way she looked, and with $5,000 in savings, she launched Spanx.

In 1998, Blakely was a one-woman shop competing in an industry dominated by large (and largely male) players. These established brands were not thinking from the customer's perspective as Blakely had been. This was her critical asset. She collected insights from her own experience. Courageously, she also sought feedback from her peers and stakeholders as she developed her product. As she has advised other would-be entrepreneurs, "Don't solicit feedback on your product, idea, or your business just for validation purposes. You want to tell the people who can help move your idea forward, but if you're just looking to your friend, co-worker, husband, or wife for validation, be careful. It can stop a lot of multimillion-dollar ideas in their tracks in the beginning."[21] Critically, Blakely understood the power of the outsider's perspective. "Don't be intimidated by what you don't know," she counseled. "That can be your greatest strength and ensure that you do things differently from everyone else."[22]

---

21   "Spanx Startup Story," Fundable.com, accessed September 11, 2017, at https://www.fundable.com/learn/startup-stories/spanx.

22   Ibid.

Like Spade, Blakely trusted her instincts—and her insights. Legend has it that while negotiating department store distribution deals, Blakely met with a buyer who didn't understand the product's appeal or functionality. Blakely took her into the ladies' room. "This is me without Spanx," Blakely intoned. Then, to demonstrate, she put the garment on beneath her clothes. "And this is me with them," she declared. The buyer immediately changed her tune. Fast forward fifteen years, and Blakely, who retained complete ownership of her company, was worth more than $1 billion.

BEST BUY

Around 2012, Best Buy seemed destined for the retail cemetery, following the fate of Circuit City and RadioShack. Amazon was steamrolling big-box retailers across the country with its selection, delivery, and pricing. To survive, Best Buy needed to reinvent itself.

In 2013, Best Buy's chief executive, Hubert Joly, initiated a five-year turnaround. The first step for Joly and his team was to get a grip on the expectations and needs of their customers and employees.

Best Buy's customers wanted price matching, stronger customer service, speedier delivery, and a better online experience. So Best Buy, with Joly at its helm, set out to deliver on these fronts. Although price matching can be expensive, Joly recognized that it would keep customers in the store and prevent Best Buy from losing sales to competitors. Joly and his team also expanded the role of the store's popular Geek Squad to reshape its customer service. In addition to approaching the Squad with questions in-store, customers could now hire Best Buy's army of tech experts to install appliances, mount televisions, or set up audio systems post-purchase. Best Buy added an element of human touch by debuting its free In-Home Advisor program to provide pre-purchase consultations. The company also invested in employee training programs to ensure staff could answer customers' inquiries across an array of products.

In addition to these in-store efforts, Best Buy revamped its online ordering experience. Instead of using a centralized warehouse system to fulfill online orders, Best Buy started shipping directly from its stores to shorten its delivery times. The company also began offering customers the option of ordering items online and picking them up in-store. These simple shifts helped Best Buy meet its customers' desire for immediate gratification. Today, nearly 40 percent of Best Buy's sales are shipped or picked up at the store.[23]

23   Kevin Roose, "Best Buy's Secrets for Thriving in the Amazon Age," *New York Times*, September 18, 2017, accessed May 6, 2018, at https://www.nytimes.com/2017/09/18/business/best-buy-amazon.html.

During the years prior to its turnaround, Best Buy was experiencing high rates of employee turnover. When the company assessed its employees' interests, it found that its team members wanted the electronics giant to reinstate its employee discount program and provide more opportunities for team members to act as customer advisors. In response, Best Buy not only reinstated the employee discount program, but it also rolled out customer-centric employee education programs. Joly credits this effort, in particular, with improving the experiences of both audiences. "The associates in our stores are much more engaged now," Joly beamed, "much more proficient."[24] Since making these critical changes, the company's annual employee turnover rate has declined from between 50 and 55 percent to 30 percent.[25]

Refocusing on the customer and employee experience has enabled Best Buy to avoid the retail graveyard and to better compete with its rivals, including Amazon. Joly has since indicated he plans to deepen the company's focus on customer and employee-related insights.

24　Ibid.

25　Nandita Bose, "Best Buy CEO Says Turnaround Done, Room to Compete with Amazon," Reuters.com, March 9, 2018, accessed May 6, 2018, at https://www.reuters.com/article/us-best-buy-ceo/best-buy-ceo-says-turnaround-done-room-to-compete-with-amazon-idUSKCN1GL2Y8.

COMPANIES THAT HAD INSIGHTS...BUT FAILED TO LEVERAGE THEM

KODAK

You may be surprised to hear that the digital camera was invented in 1975—by Eastman Kodak.

That year, 24-year-old Steve Sasson presented his new technology—the all-electronic camera that used no film, paper, or consumables—to Kodak executives. Sasson said he was sure digital cameras could compete in the consumer market against the 110- and 135-film cameras, particularly because digital technology could allow photographers to display images on their television sets. Sasson even suggested the images could one day be conveyed over telephone lines.[26]

The executives pushed back hard on Sasson. For one thing, they wanted to protect Kodak's existing revenue streams. At the time, Kodak profited at every step of the traditional photographic process, from the click of the camera's shutter to the burst of a flashcube to the local photo shop or drug store that printed images on Kodak paper. For another thing, Kodak executives disagreed that digital formats would significantly disrupt the market. As

---

26 James Estrin, "Kodak's First Digital Moment," *New York Times*, August 12, 2015, accessed August 31, 2017, at https://lens.blogs.nytimes.com/2015/08/12/kodaks-first-digital-moment/?mcubz=1.

Sasson put it, "They were convinced that no one would ever want to look at their pictures on a television set."[27]

Ultimately, Kodak secured the patent for Sasson's technology, which it held until 2007. The patent generated billions for Kodak, but it wasn't enough to keep the company afloat. Although Kodak eventually entered the digital camera market, it waited until it was too late. Kodak filed for bankruptcy in January 2012.

A&P

Founded in 1859, the Great Atlantic & Pacific Tea Company, better known as A&P, was an American icon for 150 years. According to the *Wall Street Journal*, A&P "was as well known as McDonald's or Google is today" and the "Walmart before Walmart."[28] From 1915 until 1975, A&P was the largest grocery retailer in the United States. Until 1965, it was the largest US retailer of any kind.[29] After filing for bankruptcy in 2010, the company officially ceased operating in 2015.

---

27 Ibid.

28 Mike Spector, "Everything You Need to Know about the A&P Bankruptcy," *Wall Street Journal*, December 13, 2010, accessed August 31, 2017, at https://blogs.wsj.com/deals/2010/12/13/everything-you-need-to-know-about-the-ap-bankruptcy/; Dave Kansas, "A&P Heading to the Checkout Counter?" *Wall Street Journal*, December 10, 2010, accessed August 31, 2017, at https://blogs.wsj.com/marketbeat/2010/12/10/ap-heading-to-the-checkout-counter/.

29 Marc Levinson, *The Great A&P and the Struggle for Small Business in America* (New York: Hill & Wang, 2011), 69.

During the early and middle parts of the twentieth century, A&P's business model of offering a vast assortment of foods at reasonable prices satiated Americans' hunger for frugality. But as Americans became more affluent in the second half of the twentieth century, they began to demand bigger stores that offered comprehensive shopping experiences. A&P no longer fit in an era when time-crunched Americans sought "superstore" conveniences such as in-store bakeries and banks.

In response, A&P opened a new test store called Golden Key. Golden Key experimented with non-A&P brand products and new departments. The store also gave its managers the freedom to get closer to customers and to offer a larger variety of products that made Golden Key into a modern "one-stop shop."

Sure enough, Golden Key succeeded. Customers reported that they preferred this new model to A&P's traditional one. It seemed A&P had discovered why it was losing market share and how it could turn things around. Now A&P needed to execute on its insight. But A&P management refused to adapt their old model to Golden Key's. They closed their Golden Key stores and chose to have their A&P stores compete on price alone. This crippled the company's ability to grow, and its margins plummeted.

In the meantime, competitors such as Kroger embraced the "superstore" model. Kroger systematically adapted every single store to the one-stop model until its entire system was rebuilt. Kroger's decision to transform itself catapulted its earnings for 25 years. Its stock outperformed the market by a factor of 10. By 1999, Kroger was the number one grocery chain in America, and A&P was headed for its end.

COMPANIES THAT NEEDED INSIGHTS...BUT FAILED TO UNCOVER THEM
NEW COKE: A CLASSIC EXAMPLE

New Coke may be the best cautionary tale for brands skeptical about the value of insights. A fixture in the beverage industry for a century, by 1985, Coca-Cola was losing market share to a variety of non-cola and diet drinks. When market research indicated people preferred the sweeter taste of Pepsi, the Coca-Cola Company decided to revamp its flagship product, proclaiming the drink the "new taste of Coca-Cola."

In taste tests, what came to be known as "New Coke" beat out both "Classic Coke" and Pepsi. The majority of participants said they were likely to consistently choose the newly formulated Coke over other options. But a vocal minority made clear that they were upset by the change and felt alienated from the brand.

Coca-Cola launched the new version in April 1985, backing it with advertising campaigns and live events throughout the country. At first, the product did well, particularly in the Northeast. Soon, however, a backlash began to take hold. This was particularly pronounced in the Southeast, where the company had its headquarters (Atlanta). Several national figures, including Johnny Carson and David Letterman, joined in the mocking of Coke's move. Even Fidel Castro weighed in, calling New Coke a sign of American capitalist decadence.[30] Across the country, New Coke became the product people loved to hate. By July, the classic formulation was back in production.

The insight Coca-Cola missed was that its customers would resent having a much-loved and long-standing product taken from them. Coke drinkers didn't like being asked to give up something they already liked, and they *really* didn't like losing a choice they previously had.

Had Coca-Cola Classic remained in production, the snafu perhaps could have been avoided. But Coca-Cola's senior management had rejected the option of introducing New Coke as *an* option rather than *the* central option, arguing that it would dilute the brand. They had failed to account for the power of habit and consumer attachment. They'd

30 Mark Pendergrast, *For God, Country and Coca-Cola: The Definitive History of the Great American Soft Drink and the Company that Makes It* (New York: Basic Books, 2004).

ignored these factors that many testers had vigorously pointed out.

UNITED AIRLINES

For individual customers, United Airlines offers an array of loyalty programs, ranging from Silver to Premier 1K. In addition to these, the airline also manages a corporate invite-only program, Global Services. In my view, Global Services diminishes the benefits of United's individual-customer programs.

The principle of United's individual-customer programs is simple: members receive benefits according to the number of miles per year they fly. To enroll in the Premier 1K program, customers must travel a whopping 100,000 miles per year. And they do. Loyal flyers are known to book a trip to Asia just to make their 100,000-mile quota. In fact, this practice is so common that it has its own name: "mileage run."

Now, you might scoff at the annoyance of an annual "mileage run." But when you're racking up your last miles, it's hardly annoying; it's fun. If you fly 100,000 miles or more per year, you almost certainly take too few vacations. So you treat a mileage run as a convenient excuse to travel. You get excited at the prospect of an impromptu weekend in Dallas—or a whole week in Asia. And you can justify it as saving money in the long run.

Global Services is a different animal. Global Services invites only go to people working for big corporations who file expenses for approximately $30,000 or more in flights per year. Sure, these customers spend a lot, but they *have* to spend it somewhere. And frankly, they're not spending their own money, so they have little or no incentive to remain loyal. What happens when they leave their employers? Their jobs end, and their travel perks end, too. They haven't paid for the rewards they've earned, so they see no reason to keep flying. The Global Services program doesn't inspire people to go on revenue-generating mileage runs in the same way as the individual Premier 1K program does.

Worse, in my opinion, than the Global Services program's misaligned incentives is United's strategy to devote additional resources to the Global Services program at the expense of the individual loyalty initiatives. In various ways, the airline now asks individual rewards members to spend more while providing them with less.

In prioritizing corporations—the target market for the Global Services program—United is neglecting the fundamental insight into human behavior that makes rewards programs work: everyone wants to be part of a club. Loyal flyers are willing to pay to belong, but they want the emotional and practical rewards of membership. They want to feel good about taking mini-vacations to reach their mileage quota, and they want to feel good about the airline that encourages them to do so.

Although it may cater more than other airlines to corporate customers, United is hardly alone in its drive for quarterly earnings. This quest routinely causes companies to lose touch with what they *know* to be true about their customers. It also causes them to miss valuable *insights* into what motivates their customers to act, what makes experiences valuable to them, and what ensures their loyalty.

INSIGHTS AND COMPETITIVE ADVANTAGE

Every brand utilizes consumer insights differently. But as we have discussed, the brands that benefit most from insights are those that *actively pursue* them. They don't stand by passively, waiting for potentially game-changing (or game-ending) *aha!* moments to reveal themselves. As we have seen, brands that are open to discovery and challenge put themselves in the best position to thrive.

Insight-searching is a race. With more and more brands leveraging the affordable insight tools at their disposal, you must get out in front of the pack. Once you make it a priority to generate insights and consistently engage in practices that help you do this, you become an insight-finding machine. You begin to discern patterns among facts, observations, and larger trends. Then you start to see the opportunities they reveal. Iteration, innovation, differentiation, and increased customer engagement all become part of what you do every day. And your brand becomes all the more agile and dynamic for it.

CHAPTER TWO TAKEAWAYS

- Cultivate empathy, curiosity, and vision to collect and harness the insights all around you.
- Rely on consumer insights for market discovery and differentiation. Trust that consumers know best.
- Dig deeper—internally *and* externally—to get to the *why* that keeps customers and employees coming back to your company.
- Make chasing insights a habit. The more often you seek insights, the better you'll become at it, and the more resilient your brand will become.

CHAPTER THREE

|

|

↓

DIGITAL VS. BIZ

The enterprise that does not innovate inevitably ages and declines. And in a period of rapid change, such as the present, an entrepreneur period, the decline will be fast.

PETER DRUCKER

The world of commerce is divided into two spheres: the physical sphere and the online sphere. Or as I call them, the "biz" and "digital" environments.

The biz sphere is the one in which we all live. It's the one where brick-and-mortar businesses provide us with a variety of products, services, and experiences. It's also the sphere with which those of us over age 40, including the majority of corporate decision makers, are most familiar and comfortable. Unlike our millennial counterparts, we did not grow up online, and we are unlikely to ever be as immersed in the digital sphere as they are. But even millennials seek out the tangible comforts the biz world can provide, including the ability to interact directly with the products they're buying and the people who are selling those products.

Just like the biz world, the digital world is a center of modern commerce, and businesses compete with one another within and across the two worlds. While people of all ages interact with brands online, companies that prioritize the digital world tend to target millennials, who grew up in the digital age and are comfortable making major purchasing decisions online. Many digital businesses have grown up online alongside their young customers. Warby Parker, an online retailer of prescription glasses and sunglasses, and Casper, an online seller of sleep products, are two notable examples.

Statistically speaking, the physical sphere of commerce should now be in decline. With baby boomers retiring and losing their purchasing power while millennial customers are coming of age and building theirs, it seems only a matter of time before digital rules the day.

Although there is ample basis for this assumption, the reality is more complex. Brands' opportunities do not lie exclusively in either the physical or the digital sphere. Rather, they are to be had where these spaces intersect.

Many of the world's most successful brands are working to bridge these worlds. As Gillette scales its online sales, Amazon is building physical stores in cities across the country. At Amazon Go locations, customers can inspect or try the items they're interested in and avoid standing in line to purchase them. Amazon Go carts scan customers' items and charge them via an app.

Amazon is not the only company blending the best elements of online shopping with the physical interaction consumers crave. Kroger offers its Scan, Bag, Go service in 400 stores across the country, and Sam's Club has launched a similar program.

Of all the brands that capitalize on these dual-sphere opportunities, though, Uber may do it best. People use Uber in the physical world, of course. But the company's disruption of the ground transport industry is rooted in what it's doing in the digital sphere. Uber makes the process of ordering a ride seamless via its app. Riders don't need to worry about carrying cash or even a credit card. Uber has totally cut out the hassle of finding a free cab and waving it down. The app does it all: tracking the approaching driver and updating you on his or her progress.

Now, thanks to Uber's innovations, companies that ask passengers to stand on street corners hoping an empty cab comes by are struggling to compete. Few saw the disruption of Uber coming, but its founders understood that where the physical and digital worlds meet, tremendous opportunity awaits.

Ultimately, the power of the digital world resides not only in its ability to make consumers' lives easier but also in its ability to facilitate interpersonal connection. Any given app is nothing more than a platform for connection. Some are better for group chats, others for image sharing, and still others for person-to-person services, including ride sharing and food delivery.

Quite simply, the digital world's instant connectivity is an improvement on what humans have sought from the physical world. That's why companies that facilitate it are succeeding. They're taking existing human patterns and leveraging them in ways that make the user's experiences not only better, easier, and cheaper but also operational on a global scale.

DIGITAL'S EXPANSIVE SCOPE

Just a decade ago, maintaining a Wi-Fi connection on the go, wherever we went, seemed impossible. Now, for the majority of us, it's inconceivable *not* to be online throughout the day, whether we're at home or out in the world. Fully participating in the digitally dominated world requires learning not only new skills but also a new way of thinking. For those of us over 40, this can seem unnecessary, difficult, and downright unappealing. Plenty of cultural influencers and corporate decision makers proudly proclaim, "I'm not on Facebook, and I never will be. I'm just not into social media"—a sentiment many understand and sympathize with. Opting out of the social media game is a perfectly fine life choice. But when it comes to sustaining a successful business, participating in social media is a must.

THE TRUTH OF SOCIAL MEDIA

Despite social media's downsides including negativity and privacy concerns, consumers continue to use these platforms to engage with brands. These represent the modern (and much more public) version of writing letters of praise or condemnation. Therefore, brands need to treat social media-based interactions as opportunities to build their understanding of their customers and those customers' perceptions of their brand.

The reality is, people are having conversations about your brand online right now. They'll continue to do this whether you want them to or not, and ignoring their online exchanges is far more dangerous than ignoring critical letters would be.

Some brands act surprised when social media storms

erupt around them. In most cases, however, those storms had been brewing for days or longer. Engaging sooner rather than later can give brands increased control over the narrative and help them prevent or mitigate the havoc an undesirable story can wreak.

A cautionary tale comes from the airline industry. In spring 2017, United Airlines came under fire for forcibly removing a ticketed and seated passenger from a flight and significantly injuring him in the process. Overbooking was to blame, a statistically driven practice that United and other airlines use to maximize profits. A flood of negative press and social media-based anger flowed from the incident, and according to many, CEO Oscar Munoz's public apology came too late to stem the tide of public hostility. Ultimately, the airline's brand—not to mention its shareholders—paid dearly.

WORKING WITH SOCIAL DATA

Believe it or not, social media sentiment can be quantified. Brands that do this gain a more comprehensive understanding of their customers, tying geographical and cultural demographics together with their customers' decision-making methods and purchasing behaviors. This quantitative data may either complement or undercut the qualitative data gleaned from customer conversations.

Many quantitative social data-gathering tools can deliver

real-time feedback about the user experience your app or website provides. You can then apply decision-making models like A-B testing to suss out exactly what your audience wants. You might, for example, create two icons for your app to find out which one users prefer.

The Obama campaign used A-B testing tied to social media data to great effect, presenting variations of its message to different markets and then fine-tuning them based on users' responses. In fact, the campaign's A-B testing initiative was so successful that the individual who ran it went on to found Optimizely, a company dedicated to helping brands personalize their customer experiences across numerous digital touchpoints.

There is no "right" way to gather quantitative data. Finding the tools that work best for you is likely to be a process of trial and error. Along the way, you will learn more about your brand and your consumers, adding to the broader knowledge base on which your insights ultimately rely.

DATA AND PRIVACY

But what about privacy? Don't consumers resent ceding so much information regarding their lifestyles, purchasing behaviors, preferences? Surprisingly, for years, the answer has been no. In the digital age, many consumers accept certain intrusions into their personal lives in order to do business in the digital sphere. For many people, connecting with whomever they wish to whenever they want to from wherever they are, often at little or no cost, is worth giving up some amount of personal information. However, most consumers are unaware of exactly how much of their behavior and preferences is being tracked and shared.

In our connected world, anything you do or don't do is captured, recorded, and analyzed. When you watch television, surf the web, go for a workout, snap pictures, or just sit in traffic, you leave a digital footprint. Taken together, your footprint represents an increasingly prized resource. Recently, *The Economist* called personal data "the world's most valuable resource" ahead of oil.[31]

Yet, as the value of personal data grows, so does the possibility of its theft or misuse. As a result, consumers are beginning to demand more control and knowledge of how companies are using their data. Many feel companies can do more to protect it.[32]

Consumers expect brands to be good stewards of their

---

31   *The Economist*, "The World's Most Valuable Resource Is No Longer Oil, but Data," Economist.com, May 6, 2017, accessed May 2, 2018, at https://www.economist.com/news/ leaders/21721656-data-economy-demands-new-approach-antitrust-rules-worlds-most- valuable-resource.

32   Steve Olenski, "For Consumers, Data Is a Matter of Trust," *Forbes*, April 18, 2016, accessed June 18, 2018, at https://www.forbes.com/sites/steveolenski/2016/04/18/ for-consumers-data-is-a-matter-of-trust/#61725f8378b3.

data. Someone may be fine with a company tracking her on-site purchases, but she may become upset when it sells or shares that data with someone else. People want to like and trust the brands they do business with. They want to believe that at some level, brands have their best interests at heart. Consumers understand that participating in the digital sphere comes with advantages and disadvantages, but they still expect to be treated with dignity and respect. Specifically, they expect brands to request their permission to share their own data. Wise companies responsibly use the quantitative consumer data they collect to innovate and grow without abusing the privilege of their customers' trust. No brand can afford to erode that most valuable asset: its customers' trust.

INSIGHTS LIE WHERE WORLDS COLLIDE

As the scope and scale of the digital world continues to grow, it causes us to question and challenge the ways in which we interact with the physical realm. Insights such as Uber's that drive industry-disrupting innovations await discovery in the space between the two worlds.

Take Google Maps, which has profoundly changed how we navigate from point A to point B. While some people used to carry around GPS devices, Google Maps now lives in everyone's pockets. Travelers can use Google Maps to plan a train ride, a day hike, or a cross-country road trip. Whatever mode of transportation they choose, Google arms travelers with all the information they need to go the distance, including estimated travel time and potential road (or subway) blocks along the way. A better, faster, cheaper way to receive directions that also makes travel easier? This is what consumers wanted. Google understood this and what enhanced digital technology could deliver, and as a result, it debuted a disruptive—and extremely popular—service.

Now, mapmakers may not love Google Maps, but there's no question that Google delivers a better product. As much as you may be tempted to see digital's expansion as a threat to your own industry, try instead to see the opportunities. Remember that exploratory thinking about how digital can transform real-world experiences opens the door to insights and, ultimately, to opportunities for meaningful innovation.

As a brand, ask yourself, "Why *are* we doing things this way? Of all the possible options, is this the best one? If not, how can technology help us get there?" Combining inquisitive thinking with a desire to improve your brand's performance can help you facilitate continuous innovation.

Entertaining a contrarian perspective may sound simple enough. But *adopting* it rarely comes easily for established brands. It's hard for them to say, "To hell with the rules.

I want to break them. I think things can be done better."
But productive dissatisfaction with the status quo is key
to uncovering groundbreaking, differentiating insights.

CONNECTING AND CONVERSING IN THE DIGITAL WORLD

Social media, like the rest of the internet, is about two
things: connecting and conversing. Since the biggest
players in this space were born, the purpose of social
media has been to help people share thoughts, ideas,
and moments with their friends at home and their peers
around the world.

When brands entered the social media game, they sought
to scale these connections and conversations. At first, a
successful piece of content was one that drew 500,000
views. Then 1,000,000 views became the standard. Then
10,000,000. Soon, it became a competition: "How many
likes will *their* Facebook post get?" brands wondered, jeal-
ously checking other brands' metrics against their own.

Although it's tempting to focus on the number of views,
hits, or likes your brand racks up, doing so misses the point
of social media. Unlike traditional advertising, a one-
way mode of communicating, social media is interactive.
In using it, you are not merely hoping that X number of
television show watchers, magazine readers, and subway

riders see and remember your image or video. Rather, you are looking to draw viewers and followers into an ongoing interaction—one they *also draw others into*. You are looking to engage your followers in such a way that they are not only entertained but also keen to share what you're doing within their own networks.

Think about it: If you were given a choice between having a million viewers or a quarter-million active fans, which would you choose? I would take the active users. After all, they have an ability to reach potential customers I do not.

That's why when it comes to social media, brands need to think beyond the mere accrual of views. They need to think about delivering content that is engaging and, when possible, useful. They need to think about starting conversations via content that users or followers want to *share*.

Therein lies the key to social media: making sure your message reaches people who *you don't know are out there* looking for the product, service, or experience you offer, and who may not know they are looking for you. Study after study shows that consumers heavily rely on peer recommendations for their purchasing and brand loyalty decisions.[33] Social media is the best vehicle for dispersing

---

33 TapInfluence and Influitive, "Influencers vs. Advocates: What's the Difference?" tapinfluence. com, accessed June 18, 2018, at http://pages.tapinfluence.com/hs-fs/hub/256900/ file-2517585402-pdf/Influencers_vs._Advocates_-_Whats_the_Difference_eBook_Final_v2.pdf.

these. Remember the $4,500 Dollar Shave Club video? Yes, it was an advertisement, but it was engaging and funny; it hit a nerve. People shared it not because it educated people about shaving or razors but because of the experience it created. Sending it to friends meant sharing a laugh, so people sent it millions of times. This is social media's unique value proposition.

Once you've moved away from an advertising-oriented perspective, the next step is to familiarize yourself with how people use the various social media outlets on which your brand should have a presence. People use Facebook, Twitter, Instagram, and Snapchat for different reasons and in different ways. Some of these platforms are text-based; others are more visual. The particular ways in which people relate to and use different social media outlets influence their sharing habits. Twitter users might be inclined to share a piece of content Instagram users would not. Examining each outlet's most popular posts can help you discern what kind of content works best on each one.

Whatever your social media strategy, remember this: It is not enough to share a single piece of content on several platforms at once. In order to maximize the business value of social media, you must strategize and curate your content according to the unique opportunities each outlet offers. Format matters. Timing matters. Trending topics matter, as do trends in user behavior. No matter which outlets you work with, you should keep a pulse of its users and your fan base by following what they see, say, and share. Flawed execution can make any campaign fall flat—or worse.

CASE STUDY: DOVE'S CAMPAIGN FOR REAL BEAUTY GETS UGLY

In 2004, Unilever (Dove's parent company) launched the Dove Campaign for Real Beauty. Intended to celebrate the natural variation among women's bodies, the campaign featured print and television ads, as well as videos, photography exhibits, a series of workshops, a book, and even a play. For years, the campaign was a big win for Dove. Several observers noted that Dove had hit just the right note about women's beauty, which is that it comes in all shapes and sizes.

Then in early 2017, Dove announced a United Kingdom-based promotion: a collection of body washes sold in bottles of different shapes. Some were taller; some were shorter. Some were round; others rectangular. According to the company's website, "From curvaceous to slender, tall to petite, and whatever your skin color, shoe size or hair type, beauty comes in a million different shapes and sizes. Our six exclusive bottle designs represent this diversity: just like women, we wanted to show that our iconic bottle can come in all shapes and sizes, too."[34] Although the company's intention seemed to be to reinforce the idea that beauty can come in different shapes and sizes, what it did instead was reconfirm—in a negative sense—that shape *matters*.

34 Linsday Lowe, "Dove's New 'Body-Positive' Bottles Spark Controversy—And Lots of Jokes," Today.com, May 9, 2017, accessed September 12, 2017, at https://www.today.com/series/love-your-body/dove-s-new-real-beauty-bottles-spark-backlash-t111327.

Via social media and more traditional outlets, backlash against the campaign came at Dove quickly and furiously. As one female brand strategist noted, "This is a naval-gazing [sic] marketing exercise that patronizes women rather than celebrates them. The shapes invite shoppers to judge themselves against what others look like, which surely increases the sense of feeling different rather than acceptance."[35] Online commenters also joined in: "Life pro tip, guys," one noted. "Don't buy a bottle for your girlfriend or wife and say that it matches her shape."[36]

In just one campaign, Dove undid more than a decade's worth of positive PR. Although the theory behind the bottle launch was consistent with the campaign, Dove's execution made all the difference. Dove (and Unilever) had myriad resources at their disposal for predicting how this initiative would be received. Running online focus groups, for example, or testing ads featuring the differently shaped bottles could have spared Dove an embarrassing public gaffe that undermined its decade-strong strategy.

In today's media environment, consumers' perceptions of a brand can change in an instant. This is why it is critical to stay on top of who is using each outlet, what they're sharing, and how others are reacting to it.

BALANCING THE DIGITAL AND BIZ WORLDS

As you negotiate these parallel worlds, consider Western

---

35 Sarah Benson as quoted in Linsday Lowe, "Dove's New 'Body-Positive' Bottles Spark Controversy—And Lots of Jokes," Today.com, May 9, 2017, accessed September 12, 2017, at https://www.today.com/series/love-your-body/dove-s-new-real-beauty-bottles-spark-backlash-t111327.

36 "Dove Soaks in Controversy with Bottles that Look like Different Body Types," Isitfunnyoroffensive.com, May 13, 2017, accessed September 12, 2017, at https://isitfunnyoroffensive.com/dove-soaks-in-controversy-with-bottles-that-look-like-different-body-types/.

versus Eastern medicine. Western medicine tends to be more symptom-focused, whereas Eastern medicine tends to address an illness's underlying causes. If you have a cold, Western medicine will prescribe a decongestant to treat your stuffed-up nose, whereas Eastern medicine will suggest strengthening your immune system. Get more sleep, an Eastern practitioner may tell you.

The best way to treat your cold likely combines both recommendations. When you just need to breathe through your nose, a decongestant is what you need. But you should also build your immune system to shore up your body's viral defenses.

Despite such dualities, we generally think in binary terms. To us, things are either left or right, black or white, right or wrong. Often, however, the best solutions are amalgamations of multiple approaches.

Balancing the digital and biz aspects of your business requires a similarly multifaceted approach. If you run a brick-and-mortar business, going entirely digital could be devastating. Whether your brand needs this biz element depends on the experience your customers are looking for and on the one that fits your brand promise. Scores of observers said Apple was crazy to open up retail stores, but many Apple fans love to go to the Genius Bar to talk to somebody when they need to fix or replace a device. In the end, you must decide what experience you want to deliver in order to balance your brand's digital and biz presences. Remember, too, that your formula needs to change with the market. That's what innovation is all about. And to adapt alongside the market, you need insights.

CHAPTER THREE TAKEAWAYS

- Don't despair at the digital world's growth. Look to the space between the digital and biz worlds for innovation opportunities.
- Leverage digital analytics technologies, such as social media sentiment tools, to acquire quantitative data more quickly, easily, and cheaply than ever before. Combined with qualitative findings assembled from focus groups and other conversations, this information can drive continual insight generation and innovation.
- Use personal data—the "oil" of the digital era—responsibly. Consumers understand they must share their data to enjoy today's online services, but they punish companies that abuse their generosity.
- Don't get hung up on social media's exposure metrics. If you strive for engagement, exposure will follow.
- Look to your customers' needs and your brand's promise to balance the digital and biz worlds. There is no one-size-fits-all formula for this, and there never will be.

CHAPTER FOUR

↓

THE ERA OF EXPERIENCES

The customer's perception is your reality.

KATE ZABRISKIE

In today's world, consumers have more choices and less time than ever before. They seek out not only reliable and valuable products and services but also quality *experiences*.

A consumer's experience with your brand extends beyond the functionality of your product or service to every point of contact—be it for sake of engagement, education, or support—with your company. It reaches from the moment she opens your door (or your website) to the moment she "buys in" to her troubleshooting call months after purchase. Even after she has consumed your product or service, your interactions with her via email or social media influence her future buying decisions.

But how can brands execute well at each stage of a consumer's experience? Well, they first need to understand what the consumer is looking for.

WE SEEK EXPERIENCES

We are drawn to experiences for one simple reason: they are our best tools for learning about the world around us. Consider for a moment how much better experiences are than rote instruction at teaching us valuable lessons. We don't remember our parents telling us not to touch the stove; we remember the burn we received when we confirmed it for ourselves. This tendency follows us into adulthood. How often do we try to save others from pain and suffering with our own hard-earned advice? And how often do they disregard our warnings? We've all heard a friend or loved one say, "You know, after I tried it myself, I realized you were right."

Experiences have this unique power to teach because they impact the way we think and feel. We crave this impact even when we're not aware of it. And the brands that give us what we're looking for, whether we realize it ahead of time or not, are those we come back to again and again.

Amplifying our thirst for experiences is our perceived lack of time. The less time we feel we have, the more inclined we are to act impulsively, on emotion. It's a simple matter of expediency. This means that brands are battling for an increasingly limited share of our attention. Whether it's online, on television, in taxi cabs, in doctor's waiting rooms, or even on the street, we're constantly being bombarded by messages. How do we cut through the noise? By seeking out authenticity. We home in on messages that are less transactional and more human—messages that betray a deeper understanding of our emotional needs. Why? Because the brands that connect with us through their messaging are those most likely to deliver the kind of experience we're looking for.

CONSUMERS WILL PAY UP FOR EXPERIENCES

When all else is equal, price matters. When all else it is not equal, price suddenly matters less—sometimes much less. A good experience can be priceless. At the very least, it's worth a few dollars more. Some industry researchers have claimed that by 2020, experience will outrank both price and product as a brand's key differentiator.[37]

Fine dining provides proof of this. Although the food's taste certainly plays a role in the experience, it is rarely what makes or breaks it. Diners are paying for the presen-

37   Walker Consulting, "Customers 2020: The Future of B-to-B Customer Experience," 2013.

tation, the atmosphere, and the service. Even when the taste disappoints, it is seldom the deal breaker that poor service or an unpleasant atmosphere can be.

Let's also consider air travel. Wouldn't you pay more if an airline could deliver a great experience from the moment you logged onto its website to book a flight until you touched down on the tarmac? Wouldn't its efforts to make you feel valued inspire your loyalty? Particularly following recent high-profile abuses of passenger "units," a higher fare may seem like a small price to pay for being treated with dignity and respect. Such an air travel experience might also make you more forgiving of small hiccups that would otherwise affect your airline choices.

Although it's not an airline, Zappos is a big believer in the power of great customer experiences. "We are a service company that happens to sell shoes," CEO Tony Hsieh quipped in Zappos's early days. Since then, Hsieh has repeatedly argued that superior customer service has driven Zappos's success. "Our philosophy has been that most of the money we might ordinarily have spent on advertising should be invested in customer service, so that our customers will do the marketing for us through word of mouth," Hsieh explained in an interview with *Harvard Business Review*.[38]

---

38   Tony Hsieh, "How I Did It: Zappos' CEO on Going to Extremes for Customers," *Harvard Business Review*, July-August 2010, accessed September 10, 2017, at https://hbr.org/2010/07/how-i-did-it-zapposs-ceo-on-going-to-extremes-for-customers.

Part of Zappos's appeal is its expansive selection on a site shoppers can navigate with ease. Zappos also ships customers' shoes for free, and the company makes returns free and easy. Although Zappos does the vast majority of its business via its website, it devotes significant resources to perfecting its call center. "A lot of people may think it's strange that an internet company would be so focused on the telephone, when only about 5% of our sales happen by phone," Hsieh points out. "But we've found that on average, our customers telephone us at least once at some point, and if we handle the call well, we have an opportunity to create an emotional impact and a lasting memory."[39] Zappos brings together the best of biz and digital worlds to deliver a superior customer experience. And its growth shows the sense behind its strategy. Founded in 1999, the company had $1.6 million in sales in 2000. In 2009, Amazon bought it for $1.2 billion.

ARTIFICIAL INTELLIGENCE AND CUSTOMER EXPERIENCE

Artificial intelligence (AI) is the business buzzword du jour. Currently, it's used primarily to discern patterns from large amounts of data in order to create algorithms, or "bots," that can automate tasks. Companies use AI to analyze browser behavior, email open rates, and search behavior to predict purchase behavior.

---

39 Ibid.

With AI, researchers can even replicate many of the human senses. Machines can sense temperature and touch. They can "see" and "hear" stimuli in their environments, responding to them and human beings via voice recognition software. As of this writing, however, no one knows how to replicate the power of human instinct—the so-called sixth sense.

Now, this is not to say that scientists will never figure this out. They may, perhaps even in my lifetime. But they have not yet. And it is precisely this human power of intuition—of *sensing* what another human being is thinking or feeling during an interaction—that brands need to build their customer service strategies around.

To be sure, a key driver behind business-oriented AI is the desire for speed, scale, and labor cost reduction. Labor costs are typically the largest expense for a business. Replacing humans in some jobs may be necessary. But when those jobs involve direct interaction with customers, trading people for algorithms can do a company's bottom line more harm than good.

Across industries, automated voice systems are notorious for frustrating customers. Although some organizations have developed automated systems with human-sounding voices, excellent voice recognition, and accurate call routing, most customers still prefer to deal with another human being. After all, if someone has made the effort to use the phone rather than an online interface, chances are they have a relatively complex question or request. A legendary example—again, from Zappos—involves a woman who called about returning a pair of boots she'd bought for her husband, who had died in a car accident. The customer service specialist who took her call not only facilitated the return but also sent the woman a bouquet of flowers. Remember Tony Hsieh's advice that every call is an opportunity to create an emotional impact—and a loyalty-inspiring experience.

Still, some customers will accept greater levels of automation than others. Determining their tolerance for it means engaging in conversations. What questions would they be willing to address via an automated system? How many steps would they be willing to take before they're put in contact with a human being? How long would they be willing to wait to speak with a real person? The objective of these conversations should be to balance cost-saving objectives with the experience that customers want—or demand.

CUSTOMER SERVICE: STILL A DIFFERENTIATOR

Companies' neglect of various elements of their customers' experience, particularly service and support, has conditioned many of us to expect frustrating encounters.

One study showed that when employees charged with processing customer returns opened interactions with the words, "Our policy is," customers were immediately incensed and did not allow them to finish their sentence: "Our policy is to issue a full refund."

Here's the good news: strengthening your customer experience can help you stand out from the crowd. In fact, reengineering *any* of the aspects of your customers' experience from technology to products to operations can net you new users or fans while helping you retain those you already have.

It seems simple enough: if you want good customers, then be good to them. Customer service is the one factor over which you, as a brand, have total control. Take it. It's not rocket science. Treat your customers with decency, dignity, and respect. Humanize your messaging and your customer experience, and you will stand out among your competition.

THE IMPORTANCE OF THE EMPLOYEE EXPERIENCE

Your employees are your brand's ambassadors. No matter how great your product or service, your customer experience hinges on a series of points of contact, each of which involves an employee.

Employees *want* to have positive interactions with customers. They want to treat customers as they want to be treated: with respect, dignity, and humanity. Dissatisfied customers only make employees' work more difficult, making *their* experience a negative one. The more frustrated or disempowered an employee feels, the less likely he or she is to look out for a brand's best interest. Conversely, the better an employee is treated, the harder he or she will work to establish positive emotional connections with customers.

The brands that deliver the best employee experience are those that foster an internal environment in which team members feel not only invested in the brand's success but also empowered to deliver on the promises it has made to its followers and fans. Company policies and procedures can restrict this, fostering negativity and dissatisfaction on both sides. That Zappos call center representative who sent flowers to a customer? She did not check with her supervisor first.

MAKING THE MOST OF EMPLOYEE INSIGHTS

Your employees' insights are critical for learning about both their experience and your customer experience. Again, your frontline brand ambassadors have the greatest access to the sentiments and responses of your external audience. They know whether your customers are satisfied or not with their interactions with your brand. More than this, your employees can shed light on the "softer" aspects of their customer interactions, helping you to develop a more nuanced understanding of what drives your customers' feedback and behavior. In other words, your employees are one of your greatest sources of insight.

That's why you should check in with your team often. Not every quarter or even every month, perhaps, but on a consistent basis. Consider what internal communication system would work best for this, and encourage your employees to use it.

Ideally, your employees should tell you about their encounters, positive and negative, *and* make suggestions about how to improve them. You want to hear something like, "I'm wondering if we could try X to stop Y problem from happening."

Your goal here should not be to rely on your employees' input per se but to encourage creative thinking and communication. Often, inspirational insights lie just beneath the surface. By facilitating a dialogue, you invite your employees to participate in and contribute to your company's growth. This can be one of the wisest investments you can make.

CASE STUDY: HEARTH AND TABLE OF LINCOLN CITY, OREGON

I recently visited Oregon, where I ate at Hearth and Table in Lincoln City. A modern, urban eatery known for building gourmet pizza and salads from local ingredients, the restaurant had earned top-notch reviews online.

When I arrived, I noticed that Hearth and Table had installed terminals for ordering and paying. This meant that you paid up front for your food—and your service. Although Hearth and Table's staff don't take your order, they do deliver it to you when it's ready.

When it came time to leave a tip at the terminal, I was prompted with options of 0, 10, 15, and 20 percent. This bothered me. I am happy to tip servers for their work. But I'm only happy to do this *after* they've done it. My first inclination was to leave no tip at all, but I knew this was unfair to the servers who were responsible for bringing me my meal and were counting on a gratuity. I could have used a credit card at the terminal and left cash at the end of the meal, but I had too little cash on me, and I worried that this could create a conflict with the server, who might (reasonably) assume that I didn't plan on tipping him or her at all.

In my view, this was a bad setup for both sides. Well before I'd had a chance to evaluate the dining experience Hearth and Table had to offer, I was inclined to head out the door.

Fortunately, the server behind the counter seemed to sense my ambivalence and proposed a solution. "If you'd like, you don't have to close out now," she said. "I can serve you, and we can close out later." I was impressed. The food was great and the server was helpful and attentive. I tipped her well, using my credit card as I'd planned.

"What you did was very smart," I told her about the way she'd initially approached me. Then we discussed how she'd taken note of other customers' hesitation and wanted to come up with a way to make their experience better. In the end, we agreed that she should approach customers with a slightly different version of what she said to me: "If you'd like for me to take care of you, we can close out your order later. Or if you'd prefer, we can close it out now." With this proposal, she opened up the possibility that she could serve customers in the "traditional" manner in which they tipped her for her service after she'd delivered it, or they could choose their gratuity up front and roll the dice.

A simple example, perhaps. But it goes to the heart of two points: one is that in order to continue to deliver a positive customer experience, businesses need to balance their cost-saving automations with what their users, fans, or followers are looking for. The second is that employees can be companies' best source of insight into how to strike this balance—and how to make small operational changes that can make all the difference.

CHAPTER FOUR TAKEAWAYS

- Offer an experience, not just a product or service. Today's consumers are looking to buy into movements and emotional journeys.
- Don't assume automation is always the answer. Strike a balance between deploying it to save money and delivering the humanized experience your customers are looking for.
- Differentiate yourself with superior customer service. Many other businesses have let theirs lapse.
- Recognize that your employees' experience matters— to your customers' experience, your ability to generate insights, and your bottom line.

CHAPTER FIVE

THE ERA OF BLENDING

It's easy to come up with new ideas; the hard part is letting go of what worked for you two years ago, but will soon be out of date.

ROGER VON OECH

Just as ours is the era of experiences, it is also the era of what I call "blending." This is the combining of two or more products, services, or experiences to create an entirely new offering. Blending can be a source of innovation and differentiation for any brand. Learning to do it well can help you stand apart from your peers and extricate yourself from the inevitable race to the bottom of competing on price.

But blending requires insights: insights into what consumers are looking for as well as the prevailing technological and cultural trends that might make a blended product, service, or experience desirable. In this chapter, we take a closer look at blending, including how certain trends influence its practice and what opportunities it holds out for modern brands.

CULTURAL TRENDS: CONSUMER READINESS

Innovation needs to be part of your culture. Customers are transforming faster than we are, and if we don't catch up, we're in trouble.

IAN SCHAFER

Part of consumers' penchant for blended products, services, and experiences stems from globalization. The rise of technology has made it easier and, in many cases, less expensive to experience more of the world than ever before. Free apps, including Skype, WhatsApp, and Viber, have made it possible to communicate with people all over the world in real time. The ascent of Facebook, Twitter, and other sharing sites and blogs has given people a window into what is happening in any corner of the world. Traveling to foreign countries has also become relatively inexpensive and, in most cases, relatively easy.

As an educator, I have noticed that blending is increasingly part of my students' personal lives. More and more of them have parents from different countries or continents, literally embodying the blending of cultures. These students have traveled, experienced different cultures, eaten different cuisines, and sampled different ways of life. Their very lives show the ways in which blending is influencing consumers' behaviors and preferences for certain products, services, and experiences.

In my own life, I have traveled extensively and been exposed to the various appliances, household products, cars, clothing, and other items that are popular in different countries. I've found many that I've preferred to their American equivalents. Over the years, I have collected a series of well-engineered appliances and other items. Often, they're more expensive, but they're also typically more reliable.

For consumers and brands alike, exposure to new ideas and ways of doing things inspires the blending of products or services. Increasingly, innovators and consumers are both asking, "Who says X and Y can't be combined to create a whole new offering?" In our modern environment, blending doesn't confound consumers; it intrigues and excites them.

Take, for example, the smartphone—the ultimate blender. Smartphones blend the power of a computer, a digital camera, and a phone in one device. Just two decades ago, each of these was a distinct tool that occupied its own space and role in our lives. At that time, it was difficult to conceive of a single, pocket-sized instrument that could combine all of these functionalities. But now, smartphones are ubiquitous. We take them for granted, assuming they will do what we expect them to and what we *need* them to, given our increasing dependency on them.

This is not an exclusively American phenomenon; it is a global one. At any given moment, your phone knows exactly where you are, and its internal gyroscopes know when you're in motion. It can not only help you stay in touch but also help you stay fit. Via software updates, your smartphone's functionality is constantly expanding, offering you new ways to navigate the myriad tasks that comprise your life. And you almost certainly welcome the blending this involves.

But it's not just smart devices. There's a whole world of blended products and services out there. In what follows, we take a closer look at a few standout examples.

BRANDS THAT HAVE BLENDED WELL

Brands across industries have used blending to create blockbuster innovations. In some cases, they have done this on their own, leveraging insights and technology to create new category-defying products, services, and experiences.

TESLA

More than a car, a Tesla is a new form of technology, a new way to save the planet, and a new standard for automobile performance. As a brand, Tesla has transformed what Tesla owners and non-Tesla owners alike expect from driving as well as car manufacturers. The brand exists in an entirely new category. Tesla delivers a multifaceted experience drivers have never had before.

These days, brands that invent their own categories are called outliers, rebels, or renegades. Certainly, many observers have referred to Tesla in this way. Indeed, the company is named after a man who was a disruptive inno-vator in his own right. But ten years from now, I doubt that Tesla will be an outlier. Other brands will have followed Tesla's lead. Imitation is the inevitable consequence of creating a whole new way of doing things.

TACO BELL AND DORITOS

In 2012, Doritos and Taco Bell collaborated to create Taco Bell's Doritos Locos Tacos (DLTs). At the time, Taco Bell CEO Greg Creed feared that the fast-food chain's impending fiftieth anniversary would make the brand seem too "old" to its largely twenty-something customers, so he challenged his team to innovate around the company's eponymous offering. It wasn't long before Taco Bell was considering a suggestion that seemed both out of the blue and destined for success: make Doritos into taco shells. "It was like, 'Holy crap!'" exclaimed Taco Bell's marketing director, Stephanie Perdue. "Nobody had ever done this before: turning a Dorito into a taco shell. It was just mind-blowing at the idea stage."[40] The company's food innovation expert echoed this sentiment. "[I]n all my years as a product developer, I've never seen a concept like this. The product didn't even exist yet, and already people knew this idea was going to be huge."[41]

Quickly, the two companies united their brands to develop a pilot product. After a series of focus groups, Taco Bell officially launched the DLTs. Sure enough, they were a hit. During the tacos' first ten weeks on the market, Taco Bell sold 100 million of them nationwide.[42] In 2014, *The Atlantic* called the innovation "one of the most suc-

---

40 Austin Carr, "Deep inside Taco Bell's Doritos Locos Taco," *Fast Company*, May 1, 2013, accessed September 5, 2017, at https://www.fastcompany.com/3008346/deep-inside-taco-bells-doritos-locos-taco.

41 Ibid.

42 Everett Rosenfield, "Taco Bell's Doritos Locos Tacos Are an Insanely Huge Hit," *Time*, June 5, 2012, accessed September 3, 2017, at http://newsfeed.time.com/2012/06/05/taco-bells-doritos-locos-tacos-are-an-insanely-huge-hit/.

cessful products in fast-food history."[43] And additional possibilities lay ahead. CEO Creed soon realized that the array of Doritos flavors opened up a veritable menu of options. "It's not just a product; it's now a platform—Nacho Cheese, Cool Ranch, Flamas," Creed told *Fast Company* in 2013. "We're going to blow everyone away in the next few years in terms of how big this idea and platform will become."[44] As of 2017, DLTs continued to dominate the fast-food space.

GLAD AND FEBREZE

Blending isn't exclusive to the tech and food industries, though. An example from the consumer products industry is the 2010 fusion of Glad-brand trash bags and the Procter & Gamble-owned Febreze household odor eliminator. Like the collaboration between Taco Bell and Doritos, Glad's OdorShield Bags combine the appealing aspects of each product as well as the two companies' brand recognition. The product taps into what representative participants expressed during product testing for bags bearing one or more of Febreze's most popular scents.

---

43 Sarah Yager, "How Taco Bell and Frito-Lay Put Together One of the Most Successful Products in Fast-Food History," *The Atlantic*, July/August 2014, accessed September 5, 2017, at https://www.theatlantic.com/magazine/archive/2014/07/doritos-locos-tacos/372276/.

44 Carr, "Deep inside Taco Bell's Doritos Locos Taco."

KENDALL-JACKSON AND RDV VINEYARDS

Believe it or not, many of the world's best wines are now blends. The forces driving this trend are simple: it's impossible to control grape-growing conditions, which means it's impossible to maintain any given varietal's taste. Vineyards that blend wines from multiple strains of grapes can deliver wines with consistent flavor, richness, and smoothness.

One of the most famous innovators in this space was Jess Jackson, cofounder of Kendall-Jackson. Once an attorney who helped sell wine for an alumni group, Jackson realized that by blending different varietals, he could create a quality product that ensured a stable brand experience. Jackson wasn't the first in the field to try this. He brought blending to a new commercial level, however, and he propelled blended wines to new heights of popularity and acclaim.

Another example of blending in the wine industry comes from Delaplane, Virginia, roughly 50 miles west of Washington, DC. There, entrepreneur Rutger de Vink founded RdV Vineyards. Situated on a rolling hill, de Vink's vineyard sits atop layers of granite. Thus, his grape plants have to work incredibly hard to reach ground water. Fortunately for RdV, vines become stronger as they grow longer. But even with stronger vines, Virginia's inconsistent weather still causes variation in RdV's grapes from one harvest to the next.

To compensate for this, the winemakers at RdV blend different varietals to produce the right mix. Like Kendall-Jackson, RdV blends wines with aromas, flavors, and textures de Vink feels are consistent with the company's brand—and ones that can compete on the world stage. De Vink's goal is to deliver some of the best wines in the world, and he believes that blending is the key to his success.

BLENDS ARE BUILT ON INSIGHTS

As we have discussed, brands need to continually innovate around the products, services, and experiences they deliver in order to maintain their competitive edge. Blending is an increasingly popular and original way to do that, particularly if the products, services, or experiences involved are those that consumers already value and cannot unite on their own. And like any other method of innovation, blending requires insights.

Across industries, from food and beverage to clothing to furniture to technology, blends built on insights are exciting audiences all over the world. Each of them fuses multiple cultural experiences, influences, and trends to deliver something that is neither shocking nor unpalatable. Each also relies on conversations with consumers about the experiences they're looking for. Although the inspiration behind these various innovations came from the brands themselves, conversations with users and customers have been critical to their ongoing development and staying power.

CHAPTER FIVE TAKEAWAYS

- Avoid a race to the bottom on price by building a product that is meaningfully different from its competitors. Blending is one way to do this.
- Consider the blended products, services, and experiences all around you. Ask yourself, "What products, services, or experiences can I combine to deliver an elevated and more valuable version of any of these?"
- Seek consumer input before, during, and after the act of blending to ensure consumers want what you're building.

CHAPTER SIX

↓

THE ERA OF (NOT) THINKING

Imagination is the highest form of research.

ALBERT EINSTEIN

Despite the ever-growing power of supercomputers, the human brain remains the most powerful computer in the world. In 2015, a Carnegie Mellon study that pitted the human brain against IBM's Sequoia computer found that the brain may move data around as much as thirty times faster than Sequoia. In monetary terms, the researchers mused that renting out your brain's power could earn you up to $170,000 per hour.[45]

---

45 David Nield, "Your Brain Is Still 30 Times More Powerful than the Best Supercomputers," Science Alert, August 28, 2015, accessed September 17, 2017, at https://www.sciencealert.com/your-brain-is-still-30-times-more-powerful-than-the-best-supercomputers.

Our brains are the seat of any rationality of which we're capable. But study after study shows that our internal supercomputers are susceptible to emotional influence, and technology has made us less reliant on them for creative problem solving. At the same time, technology has made it possible to cram more and more into our daily lives. Taken together, this is a recipe for reckless and emotion-driven decision making.

Unfortunately, as a society, we are not replacing lower-level thinking with higher-level thinking or contemplation; we're replacing it with entertainment. This lures us away from critical thought and into comfort and complacency. Complacency is dangerous for businesses as well as consumers. They may miss out on opportunities for learning and self-development, and companies may stagnate while hungrier, more creative, and more agile competitors come along and eat their lunch.

Businesses must "think" to innovate. Only by taking the time to engage and ponder with consumers, users, and followers can brands arrive at the insights that are central to the sort of *aha!* moments that made them strong in the first place.

In this chapter, we look at ways in which the same technologies that routinely preclude thinking can also facilitate insight-generating interactions between consumers and brands. Technology can help brands access the insights they need to craft and deliver the products, services, and experiences consumers are looking for.

THE IMPACT OF (NOT) THINKING

Modern life offers more opportunities than ever to put our thinking on hold. Take Google Maps and other GPS systems. When I was younger, I used directions and maps to get around. Now, I am reliant on Google Maps. More than the directions Google Maps provides, I love its real-time traffic information. Armed with it, I make better navigational decisions and save precious time.

Of course, there is a downside to all this. For starters, I don't know my way around New York, where I live. Nor do I know my way around any of the other cities I frequently visit nearly as well as I used to. As much as I hate to admit it, I no longer pay attention to where I'm going. This can happen to any of us, even in the places we spend the most time. When I was visiting South Korea once, my taxi driver's phone (and, with it, his access to Google Maps) died, and he had to pull over. He had no idea where he was. We were stranded.

It's not only Google Maps that creates this kind of dependency either. Name any digital platform, and you'll notice it. The more time you spend on any of them, the more you come to rely on them to help you literally or figuratively navigate your daily life.

Having researched the impact of this era of (not) thinking on individuals and brands alike, I've begun making more of an effort to reduce my dependency on technology and flex my creative-thinking muscles. When I'm traveling by car or foot, I endeavor to take different routes from point A to point B. When I stumble upon unexpected goings-on, I can sense my natural curiosity and inquisitiveness taking hold. I know that I'm making myself more and more open to observing people, places, and things from new perspectives.

I encourage you to try this, whether you do so for your own edification or as part of an insight-generating process. There are an endless number of changes you can make to your routine on any given day. Instead of always going right at a given turn, make a left. Explore. Do something different.

THINK LIKE A BUSINESS

Without a doubt, technology is a game changer for companies in every industry. But any business seeking to innovate and stand out from the crowd must avoid the complacency technology can inspire. Its leaders also need to avoid falling prey to the false belief that technology can do their thinking for them. The ability to think creatively about fulfilling the needs and desires of their audiences—internal and external—is what keeps companies "human."

Whether you're operating as a private individual or as an entrepreneurial thinker seeking to take your brand to new heights, you start thinking when you're outside your comfort zone, doing different things than you normally would. You begin to see patterns among people, places, and situations that had previously seemed unconnected. At a corporate level, this can be incredibly powerful. When you start to piece together the consumer data you've collected in different ways, you'll spot patterns and associations that may otherwise have gone unnoticed. In other words, you'll inch closer and closer to the elusive *why* that is at an insight's core.

To prime yourself to see new patterns, consider continuously exposing yourself to unfamiliar perspectives. In 2017, Facebook CEO Mark Zuckerberg committed to speaking to someone new each and every day—an approach similar to that of the corporate leaders featured on the CBS series *Undercover Boss*. The show follows high-ranking executives as they engage with frontline workers and managers who have no idea who the executives are. Going undercover in this way enables the business leaders to have conversations with company workers and be exposed to trends, practices, and challenges of which they'd previously had no knowledge. For the leaders featured in *Undercover Boss*, transformational insights often wait outside the office—*aha!* moments that begin with seeing different things and seeing things differently.

In addition to helping you discover unexpected insights, out-of-the-box thinking puts you in a better position to weather the one constant any business can rely on: change. Thinking is also the one element of your personal or business life over which you retain total control and which you may leverage to your advantage at any time, under any circumstances.

Choose to experience new things. Put yourself in situations that challenge you—that force you to keep your edge and broaden your perspective. Doing so is how you get to *aha!*

YES, TECHNOLOGY CAN HELP YOU THINK

Brands hire market researchers like me to investigate their customers' deeper motivations. Clients want to know the *why*—what motivates their customers' behaviors and decisions. All too often, however, brands end up relying exclusively on quantitative data, particularly those derived from surveys. Commonly citing budget and time constraints, brands restrict their information-gathering and analysis initiatives to "the numbers"—data that is relatively inexpensive to collect and that provides information about the *what* of a brand's performance. Despite being critical to a brand's success, quantitative analysis alone often fails to reveal the *why* behind performance figures.

Part of brands' penchant for quantitative analysis is that historically speaking, qualitative assessments were expensive to do. They required real-time individual or group conversations, conducted either in person or by phone, each of which required significant manpower. Simply recruiting the right participants was a costly effort. On top of this, focus groups were traditionally conducted during evenings after work, making it incumbent on company hosts to feed participants in addition to paying them for their time. Companies that hired outside firms to conduct focus groups had to pay these researchers' fees as well. From the moderator's time to data collection to management and analysis, the costs added up.

For all of the expenses associated with qualitative assessments, however, I have rarely encountered clients who have been satisfied with a purely quantitative approach. Fortunately, technology has made qualitative analysis faster, easier, and more affordable.

As we've discussed at various points in this book, you can pull qualitative consumer-sentiment data from social media and e-commerce sites. Through these outlets, customers can communicate with your company directly, delivering feedback regardless of whether you solicit it. You don't need to recruit people to review your brand or product via Facebook, Twitter, Amazon, or Yelp. Written comments, photos, and even videos are all likely to come your way without you doing anything at all. And if you're at a startup or small business that's considering launching a new product or service, sites such as Kickstarter can provide you not only with funding but also with powerful feedback about consumer preferences and price points.

Of course, all of this information is uncontrolled, uncontrollable, and uncurated. But you can organize and track it relatively painlessly using one of the many social listening tools on the market. These programs can clue you in to engage with your users or followers in different contexts, a practice critical to any brand's success.

Technology can also help you go beyond media monitoring to gather and assess original consumer insights faster, less expensively, and on a scale you never could before. The iResearch insights platform and other collaborative tools deliver the benefits of one-on-one conversations and focus groups to companies big and small.

GOING ONLINE WITH FOCUS GROUPS

In 1998, I founded iResearch in response to some of my

clients' frustrations around getting to the *why* underlying their audience's purchasing decisions and brand loyalty. These were my smaller clients, including some startups, and none had the deep pockets of their outsized competitors. These clients were looking for an affordable option for tapping into the rich, nuanced, and helpful feedback they knew focus groups could deliver.

I took this demand and ran with it. For years, I have facilitated focus groups for companies around the globe, so I knew what it took to do it well. There was (and is) an art and a science to it. But I thought that if I could conduct focus groups online, I could eliminate much of the expense for my cost-conscious clients. After all, I realized, most of the costs associated with in-person focus groups are logistics-based: venue, manpower, catering. I thought that if I focused on the replicable infrastructural elements of focus groups, including moderators' guides and mechanisms for data collection, then I could build a scalable, convenient, and inexpensive model.

Still, I was concerned about whether I would be able to re-create the atmosphere of a focus group—one characterized by ongoing group conversation that builds over time and out of which new ideas tend to emerge. Cautious but undeterred, I went to work. Together with software engineers, I spent years creating an online space in which clients could design, create, and conduct focus groups without compromising the rigorous standards of sound research.

Now, with the iResearch platform operational, I have found that online focus groups really do facilitate conversations as well as their offline counterparts. Akin to an exclusive cocktail party, they become engaging social events that encourage connections and conversations among strangers that leave everyone thinking, "I learned some really interesting things tonight!"

For one thing, online focus groups bring together people from anywhere in the world. Whereas traditional focus groups typically involve participants from a single geographic area, online focus groups suffer from no such limitation. For another thing, online focus groups can simultaneously accommodate comments from the client hosting the focus group, the moderator, and all of the participants. In a traditional setting, the client behind the mirror cannot interact in real time with the moderator due to the biases this might inspire among the participants. In an online environment, however, the client can interact with the moderator without being seen.

Perhaps counterintuitively, participants of online focus groups may interact with the moderator and each other even more freely than in in-person groups. In a traditional environment, the more vocal or naturally extroverted participants may deliver the lion's share of the commentary. In an online environment, anyone may contribute to the conversation at any point, regardless of who else might be doing so at the time. It is far easier for participants to type comments when they're ready than it is for them to wait for the "right" moment to jump into a group conversation. What's more, in an online environment, you can give your participants direct access to any media available via the internet. You can showcase images, video, and audio in addition to guiding participants through polling questions. Digital mailers, radio advertisements, and product demonstrations are all fair game. In a traditional environment, you could call participants' attention to just one display at a time. In an online environment, you may allow participants to continue to access whatever media you wish for the duration of a session. Having this access may deepen certain responses and the overall conversation, increasing the value of the qualitative data you're collecting.

As I observed clients of all sizes using the online focus group tool I'd created, I became increasingly aware of its value and promise. I committed to continuously improving it, and ultimately I arrived at the idea of turning it into a client-driven, on-demand platform that businesses could use anytime, from anywhere, in any language. Of course, such a significant iteration required that I build in the necessary infrastructure (live chat, media sharing, participant tracking, data collection, etc.) for clients to run online focus groups on their own. I also remained committed to keeping the platform affordable. I knew that in addition to the scale and flexibility it afforded users, the power of my platform lay in it being relatively inexpensive. That's why I made iResearch available to any insight-seeking individual or brand. Users don't need to talk to me or a salesperson to get started. They can simply sign up and start having conversations.

Today, my goal for iResearch is for it to become a go-to insight-generating tool that brands can use at a moment's notice. My deeper goal, however, is to help brands leverage technology to gather the sort of insights that drive creativity and innovation. I hope to leave a legacy of rich, engaging, and revealing conversations that result in the creation and delivery of superior products, services, and experiences.

CHAPTER SIX TAKEAWAYS

- Fight technology's temptation to think less *and* less creatively. Challenge yourself to engage more directly in the world around you. Take the long way home, introduce yourself to new people and situations, and consider matters from a series of perspectives.
- Use technologies such as social listening tools to collect and analyze online conversations about your

brand. They're going to happen regardless; you might as well learn from them.

- Turn to online insight platforms, such as iResearch, to engage in deep, cost-effective conversations with your customers next door and around the world. You'll be surprised at the *aha!* moments that you come away with.

CHAPTER SEVEN

↓

AHA! MOMENTS

Research is formalized curiosity. It is poking and prying with a purpose.

ZORA NEALE HURSTON

To uncover *aha!* moments, you cannot rely on data alone. You must engage in conversations. Qualitative feedback from your customers, followers, or users adds context and dimension to quantitative measures, elevating these from assessments of the *what* to analyses of the *why* behind consumers' choices and purchasing patterns.

Although the most productive conversations are those that have a natural flow, it is up to you as the insight seeker to steer them in valuable directions. As we have discussed elsewhere in this book, directing conversations with your audience requires you to understand their perspectives and thought processes. You must account for emotional factors, particularly the pursuit of pleasure and the fear of pain, as well as practical concerns, including price and product utility. How these factors influence your participants' responses depends on how they perceive your brand. And the only way to understand the role these play for your respondents is to *ask them*—to pose the right questions and then *listen* to what they say.

Equally important, you need to be clear on your objectives for any conversation before you enter into it. You can't expect participants to simply hand you the information you're seeking. At the same time, however, you need to remain flexible enough to maintain a relaxed conversation and take participants' responses in stride.

People want to feel heard. They take part in conversations they believe will improve the products, services, and experiences they're interested in. But the more conversations feel like work, the less forthcoming with honest, interesting, or valuable information participants will be.

Instead of worrying about how you will fit all your topics in, map out a course and use your best judgment and empathy to keep participants on track. Do this, and you will find that most or all of the important data you're looking for will emerge. Loosen your grip on your objectives enough to allow conversations to be engaging, interesting, and fun. Such conversations are always more likely to yield insights.

Regardless of what you're trying to gain from a given conversation or whom you're having it with, you must remember to listen. You cannot learn from your audience members by talking *at* them. Conversations, surveys, and focus groups are all opportunities to take information *in*, not to direct information outward in an effort to persuade your audience to buy or believe something. Think of these interactions as chances for you to get outside the office and see your brand in a new light.

CONVERSATION TOOLS
ONE-ON-ONE DISCUSSIONS

Although there are downsides to one-on-one exchanges with consumers such as their relatively high cost, there are also advantages. One plus is the opportunity to delve deeply into one person's contact with your brand. Doing so can give you explicit, detailed information about their experience. You might learn how they discovered your brand and interacted with it, what organizations they consider to be your competitors, how they chose your product or service, and how your team handled their questions or concerns. You may also happen upon a superfan: a consumer who loves what you do and knows how you could make your most loyal users' experiences *even better*.

On the other hand, you might struggle to engage an individual for an extended period. I've found that a consumer on the phone or Skype is likely to give you only 30 or so minutes. If you manage to engage someone in an impromptu exchange on the street or in a store, he or she may give you 5 minutes or less. To be sure, short conversations can be revealing, but they also offer less opportunity to achieve your objectives.

One-on-one conversations also make it impossible for the participant to play off others' ideas. As much as any given individual may know about his or her experience, hearing about others' often sparks recollections and even new ideas. Asking the participant to comment on other consumers' or fans' feedback can help, but it's not the same as a live group conversation.

If you pursue individual conversations, I recommend conducting them in person or leveraging any of the various phone, tablet, or computer-based videoconferencing apps. This technology is inexpensive or free to use, and you as the insight seeker benefit immensely from the intimacy of face-to-face exchanges.

SURVEYS

Surveys are most effective at gathering quantitative rather than qualitative data. Although surveys can ask open-ended questions, participants tend to move quickly through questionnaires. Often, they literally check the box and move on, even when the survey prompts them to deliver qualitative feedback.

With that said, surveys are the ideal tools to check your findings from individual conversations or focus groups. Especially if you want to evaluate the viability of ideas, product concepts, or marketing campaigns, surveys can help you extrapolate from smaller samples to larger populations. You can also use surveys to follow up with participants of focus groups or one-on-one conversations about comments they made regarding their experiences of your brand.

Surveys are not the panacea some in the business world seem to think they are. But they can complement qualitative analyses quite nicely. The key lies in using multiple methodologies.

FOCUS GROUPS

Focus groups are discussions involving a moderator and 7 to 12 participants. Similar to individual conversations, focus groups provide opportunities to collect qualitative feedback regarding participants' experiences and perceptions of your brand and, if you choose, those of your competitors. More than this, however, focus groups provide opportunities to test out ideas, ads, messaging, packaging, websites, and more. Whether you're seeking input on a product or service, or you're gauging the effectiveness of an advertising campaign, soliciting the opinions of users can help you make more informed decisions.

As we discussed in chapter six, the primary disadvantage of focus groups is their cost. Hosting, managing, and feeding participants can be expensive. Another potential disadvantage of focus groups is the influence of interpersonal dynamics. Are some participants less likely to speak up than others? Perhaps. Do dominant participants deliver all of the best or most useful feedback? Perhaps not.

All this said, focus groups can inspire participants to think deeply about their experiences and opinions, which can yield rich results. Group conversations often build on themselves, opening doors to new perspectives and ideas. Although it can be difficult at times to keep a group conversation on track, participants can also motivate each other to say, "Yes, exactly!" or "I had a different experience." Often, inspired individuals make meaningful and enlightening contributions they had not foreseen themselves making.

ONLINE FOCUS GROUPS

As mentioned in the prior chapter, brands now have the

option to conduct focus groups online. In addition to eliminating many of the costs associated with traditional focus groups, online focus groups also provide other advantages.

For one thing, online focus groups are not geographically limited. You can conduct a group conversation with people from North America, Europe, Australia, and Asia all at once. (Some platforms, including iResearch, support nearly any language.) Depending on your goals or your brand's reach, expanding your focus group in this way can significantly broaden its findings.

Another advantage of online focus groups concerns the collection and curation of data. For example, iResearch users can download a complete transcript of their focus group as soon as the session is complete. This transcript can be searched and sorted in various ways, facilitating immediate analysis and shortening the time lag between data collection, insight generation, and implementation.

Do online focus groups have any downsides? Well, some people assume that they must yield poorer insights than their traditional counterparts because the moderator might otherwise glean information from participants' body language and facial expressions. Once, I believed this myself. But soon after I started hosting online focus groups, I realized that participants can convey their emotions during online discussions as well—even exchanges that are entirely text-based.

Think about it: the average person conducts between 70% and 90% of their daily communications via text, email, and other digital messaging apps.[46] In the digital age, people have learned to convey their emotions through these media. In fact, online focus groups sometimes yield *more* emotion-based information than traditional ones because of the relative anonymity the chat room affords participants. In my experience, online participants tend to use language that is more direct than the language they use during traditional live conversations. Plus, participants often put more thought into written responses than they do into spoken ones, and they sometimes augment these responses with emojis and other internet shorthand. As a regular conductor of online focus groups, I can clearly make out the personality of each participant within the first 10 minutes of a session.

FOCUS GROUPS: FAQ

HOW MANY FOCUS GROUPS SHOULD WE CONDUCT?

A question people commonly ask me is how many focus groups they need to conduct in order to collect the data

---

46   Erik Kostelnik, "5 Facts about Communication in the Workplace You Need to Know," Entrepreneur.com, accessed June 18, 2018, at https://www.entrepreneur.com/article/280301.

they seek. The truthful answer is, the more focus groups, the better. No one has unlimited time or assets, however, so deciding on a reasonable number is part of the process.

I recommend a minimum of two sessions that cover the same ground. Ideally, the participant compositions should be consistent across both groups (more on that in the following "Whom Should We Recruit" section). To confirm your findings, I recommend two additional sessions that have consistent group compositions and incorporate the same questions.

WHOM SHOULD WE RECRUIT?

For each focus group session, you should recruit between 7 and 12 participants. To ensure the right number show up, confirm roughly 15. Groups of a dozen or fewer tend to interact well with one another, engaging each individual and giving him or her a chance to build on others' ideas.

Of course, groups need the right participants. The first step in your search is to delineate what you want to learn. This will guide you through such questions as: "Do I want people who are already using the product?" "Do I want people who haven't ever thought about my product before?" "Do I want people who have defected—people who once used my product or service but have moved on, perhaps to a competitor?"

The second step is to clarify desirable demographics. Think about sex, age, educational attainment, income, geographical location, and even such personal attachments as religious or political affiliations. Being clear on the characteristics your ideal participants should possess is critical. I often ask clients, "If I could deliver you the ideal one person right now that you would like to talk to, who would it be?"

You may be able to identify an appropriately sized pool of people from within your database of customers, users, or followers. If you cannot, consider casting a wider net via Facebook, Slack, Twitter, or Instagram. You may also purchase access to participants from a market research sampling company such as Critical Mix or Research Now SSI, or create and then tap into an online community composed of people who meet your criteria.

Once you've identified potential participants, the next step is to screen them. Commonly, this involves requesting that they complete a short survey to confirm that they are who they say they are and that they're interested and available to contribute. Again, in my experience, only about 50% of the people who *say* they're ready, willing, and able to join a focus group actually *do*.

SHOULD WE RECRUIT AND SELECT PARTICIPANTS BASED ON SPECIFIC CRITERIA?

In a focus group, you are looking to go *deeper*—to explore potentially fruitful lines of thought and conversation as fully as possible. In general, this means you want to avoid recruiting participants whose perspectives on or experiences with your brand significantly diverge.

One challenge associated with working with groups whose participants have divergent perspectives is that the same questions may not be equally relevant to all. Say, for example, you're interested in a product's user experience. The questions you have for users will not apply to non-users. You may be interested in conducting a focus group with non-users who are considering purchasing the product, but this group conversation will be completely different from the user-group conversation.

A second challenge of working with a varied group is that when participants' experiences or perspectives on a given product or service are at odds, a conversation can descend into unproductive disagreement or outright conflict.

Recently, I worked on a rebranding project for a national soccer team. The organization was opening a new stadium, and it wanted to modernize its logo and other brand assets without alienating the team's superfans.

Given how attached soccer fans can be to their team's look and merchandise, the rebranding effort was bound to be challenging. The team's leaders and I knew some fans would resist any change to the team's logo, but we wondered whether some would resist more strongly than others. In the end, we decided to host four focus group sessions—two among superfans and two among new fans—to gauge all participants' receptivity to the proposed changes. In order to determine who was a superfan versus a new fan, we considered potential participants' memberships in fan clubs and other groups as well as their ticket purchases. (All season ticket holders were classified as superfans.)

We believed each set of groups would present distinct perspectives and feedback. We expected that the superfans would give us an idea of the backlash we could expect, and that the newer fans would offer up some more constructive input on which aspects of the new branding were working. We conducted these focus groups online, where we were able to have deep, productive conversations with all four groups without breaking the budget.

Once we compiled our findings from the focus groups, we found a surprising number of commonalities. Many of the changes we made were actually welcomed by *both* sides. In the end, the rebranding effort reenergized the fan base and generated buzz around the new season and the team's future.

HOW SHOULD WE COMPENSATE PARTICIPANTS?

Participants should always be compensated in some way, shape, or form. Not only does it encourage them to show up, but it also reassures them that you value their time and their feedback. Remember: you want both their attention and their input. Knowing they can expect to be compensated once the session has concluded will keep them present and engaged for the duration.

In most cases, compensation should be commensurate with participants' level of interest. Consumers who are highly involved with your product or process may be eager to participate in a focus group. To these participants, compensation may be relatively unimportant, and you can offer them less without compromising your results. On the other hand, if consumers whose feedback is important to you have little or no interest in joining in your focus group, you'll need to pay them more.

Determining the right level of compensation may involve some back-and-forth with potential participants. Talk to individuals in your target group. Soon enough, they'll make their expectations clear.

CAN FOCUS GROUPS GENERATE POSITIVE PR?

Although it may not be your primary motivation for conducting one, focus groups do have PR value. Often, participants who have positive experiences become increasingly engaged in your brand and its progress. Particularly when they see you acting on their feedback, these consumers can become superfans who advocate for your brand on- and offline.

If this seems unlikely to you, I understand. It surprised me, too. But what I've learned is that when participants feel valued, they tend to gain a new level of interest in and excitement about your brand. Often, this motivates them to share their experience with others.

HOW CAN WE MAKE THE MOST OF EMPLOYEE FOCUS GROUPS?

As increasing numbers of companies realize that conversations with their internal audiences can be as important as conversations with their external ones, they're turning to online focus groups to collect input from their employees. Where traditional focus groups cannot afford the protection of anonymity, online focus groups can. Even an online focus group's moderator can remain ignorant of exactly who the participants are.

In-person focus groups don't grant participants anonymity, making them reticent to share uninhibited feedback. When conducted by an independent moderator, online focus groups do allow anonymity of participants and tend to facilitate honest feedback. I've worked with several clients who reported that internal online focus groups yielded significant and valuable information.

CHAPTER SEVEN TAKEAWAYS

- Allow a natural flow of conversation to make the most of your focus group, online or otherwise. Recognize the value of participants building on one another's responses.
- Select 7 to 12 participants for your focus group by confirming about fifteen individuals and screening out those with divergent or irrelevant experiences or opinions. Be sure to compensate participants for their time.
- Don't underestimate the brand-boosting benefits of focus groups. Participants may become superfans who then promote your brand to their peers.
- Consider hosting an internal focus group to glean employees' insights. Be sure to employ an independent moderator to facilitate honest responses.

CHAPTER EIGHT

▼

THE DIGITAL PROMISE

Our society needs more heroes who are scientists, researchers, and engineers. We need to celebrate and reward people who cure diseases, expand our understanding of humanity, and work to improve people's lives.

MARK ZUCKERBERG

The reality of the modern age is that technology has pervaded it, changing our relationship with the most fundamental aspects of our universe: time and space. Technology has enabled us to accomplish more in less time than we ever could before and to connect with people and places around the world with the press of a button.

Arguably, these are good things. The dark side of technology, however, is that it bombards us with by information and overwhelms us with choices. While technology can free up our time, it can just as quickly fill up our schedules. Many of us can't keep up with technology's barrage of messages and demands. Human beings are not wired to make choices all the time—choices about what we read and listen to, about what products and services we use. Most of the time, we make decisions on instinct. Our world moves so quickly, we cannot help it.

As much as digital innovation is facilitating and expanding human connection, it's also dividing us. How often do we hear people bemoaning the end of face-to-face and phone-based conversations, claiming they could have spared themselves and others both time and anguish if they'd just spoken in real time rather than via text, email, or Facebook Messenger?

This is the promise and the challenge of the digital age: using technology to save time without giving up on the things that truly matter. Consumers know this. And as reliant on technology as they may be, they remain invested in authentic human connection and experiences that enrich their lives. This is the space in which brands have an opportunity to stand out.

SURVIVAL IN THE DIGITAL AGE

Adapting to the realities of the digital age involves far more than simply learning to do business digitally. Although brands need to engage with the various technological forces that are influencing consumers' behavior, including social media, adapting to the realities of the digital age means leveraging technology to *deliver the experiences people are looking for*.

Consider Uber and Airbnb, for example. Uber didn't invent the concept of giving someone a ride from point A to point B any more than Airbnb invented renting rooms. What each of them did invent, however, was a new experience.

Uber not only made it easier, cheaper, and in many cases, faster to find a ride around town, but it also transformed the urban transport experience by giving users far more control over it. Uber users have information about their drivers they never did before, not the least of which is exactly where their ride is and when they can expect it to arrive. Uber's payment process is also an improvement over that of taxi companies, and Uber offers its riders the option of being transported in cars that are far more luxurious than taxis typically are.

Similar to Uber, Airbnb made the process of finding a local and paying to stay in their home easier than ever before.

But Airbnb has also transformed the vacation experience by offering its users a way to truly experience everyday life in the places they visit. In many cases, Airbnb users meet the owners of the apartments or homes they rent space in. From their hosts, Airbnb users can gain insider information about local restaurants and sights.

Neither of these billion-dollar companies owns any physical cars or rooms. Their expertise lies in the sphere of experience, and they've leveraged technology to innovate in ways that have made them two of the most popular brands in the world.

DIFFERENTIATE OR DIE

Although brands may innovate—and differentiate themselves—by creating an entirely new product or service, they may also do so by innovating around various elements of the experience they deliver. These can include pricing, payment options, customer service, and even aspects as seemingly insignificant as shipping times. What matters is choosing the right components on which to focus.

Let's consider one of the world's top contemporary innovators: Amazon. News of Amazon's latest inventions is everywhere, but one of its most significant innovations has been its ability to blend its digital ecosystem with brick-and-mortar retail spaces. In addition to opening Amazon Go locations across the country, Amazon has also acquired Whole Foods with a promise to revolutionize the way people shop for food. Time will tell whether or not Amazon's efforts pay off. What is already clear, however, is that the company trusts its observations of consumer behavior, and now, it's seizing on opportunities to expand its user base in the biz world.

KEEP THE FOCUS ON YOU

If there's one thing companies love, it's trying to one-up their peers. They often race to add features to their products or services without considering whether or not those additions actually improve the user's experience.

I'm reminded of my own experience with the real estate industry. During recent years, I have done a considerable amount of work to help property developers brand and market new urban residences. As in other industries, real estate shoppers are looking for an experience. More than an apartment or condominium, renters and buyers are looking for spaces that create a live-work-play nirvana. Amenities such as gyms, yoga studios, restaurants, bars, and even pet grooming facilities are popping up in housing complexes in every major city in America. The problem with this strategy is that having more amenities available to residents comes at a price residents must ultimately pay. Some are willing to do this; others are not. As a result, this amenity race is getting some developers into trouble.

In real estate and elsewhere, the reality is that amenities are not the only aspect of the consumer experience that provides opportunities for innovation and differentiation. Another is the leasing or purchasing process itself, which can be stressful and complicated. Developers that leverage technology and invest in customer service to make this process as smooth and easy as possible tend to stand out from their competitors.

Moving into a new home is another critical aspect of a renter's or homebuyer's experience, and it, too, provides opportunities for innovation and differentiation. Partnerships between real estate developers or brokers and brands that renters and buyers may naturally gravitate toward could benefit all parties involved. Imagine if a developer partnered with Casper and made the mattress-buying and installation process a snap for new residents. With the check of a box, a new mattress could arrive in the renter's or buyer's home. At little or no cost to the developer, the consumer gets an experiential value-add—one they're likely to share with friends—and Casper secures a new customer. Collaborations between any number of digital or brick-and-mortar providers of products and services could yield similar results.

INNOVATION AROUND MESSAGING

There are three types of messaging: paid, owned, and earned. While a brand may derive value from all of these, some of the most significant opportunities for innovation and differentiation lie in the earned space. Let's take a closer look at all three.

Paid advertising is the most traditional. It's space in a newspaper or magazine, time on radio or television airwaves, or, in the digital age, an ad on someone else's website. By its nature, paid advertising is static and one-way. Although paid ads can boost the sponsoring brand's visibility, they're becoming less effective because consumers are being constantly bombarded by ads and various other messages. Simply put, it is getting harder to capture and retain consumers' attention with traditional advertising.

Owned messaging is communication via the sponsoring brand's own website or social media channels. Often far less costly than placed ads, owned media can also drive significantly higher amounts of engagement. Especially on social media, owned messaging tends to be inviting viewers to engage directly with the brand.

Earned advertising comprises the stories, videos, or other digital posts about a brand or created by the brand itself that its fans can then share with their networks. These stories and videos can be less or more expensive to create. (Remember Dollar Shave Club's $4,500 video?) But when they strike a chord with viewers—even if they don't go "viral"—the PR generated by that earned messaging can be extremely valuable. This kind of messaging can reach people the sponsoring brand doesn't know are out there looking for its product or service. People tend to listen more closely to their peers and social connections than they do to brands themselves.

Any of these types of messaging can help build your brand awareness. But only by understanding the limitations and possibilities of each can you innovate around how you use them. Particularly in the owned and earned spaces, your viewers and followers will let you know whether your message is coming across. They may even offer up helpful suggestions for how to increase its impact and shareability.

In whatever ways you leverage each of these channels, make sure your messaging is consistent across them. In the paid, owned, and earned spaces, you need to look and sound the same. The story of who you are and why you do what you do must be as clear and persuasive in one channel as in the next. Just as consumers want to be able to predict their experiences of your brand, they also want to see consistency in your messaging. This confirms for your customers and fans that they know who you are and what you're about.

CHAPTER EIGHT TAKEAWAYS

- Leverage technology to humanize your brand and differentiate the experience it delivers to consumers. That differentiator may be your product's features, its price, its delivery method, or its integrations with other products or services.
- Make the most of the variety of media available to you in the digital age. Paid, owned, and earned advertising each has its own strengths and drawbacks.

CONCLUSION

Today's insights truly are tomorrow's facts. They hold the key to innovation, differentiation, and sustainability in our modern, technology-driven environment. For each of us, they pave the path to more satisfying, enriching experiences and interpersonal connections.

Whether you're a fledgling startup or an established brand, technology has brought insights closer to your reach than ever before. An array of affordable social media and consumer-tracking tools has made it easy for you to quantitatively assess your brand's performance. A series of digital technologies, including iResearch, has also made it cheaper and faster for you to collect vital qualitative feedback. Considered together with the backdrop of the larger, macrolevel trends driving consumer behavior, all of this data can supercharge insight generation within your organization.

So why do so many brands continue to struggle to generate the insights they need? As the head of strategy at a packaged-goods company explained, "We have for far too long had insight staff sitting in the back seat of the car criticizing the journey. In fact, they need to be in the front seat where they can see the road and help the driver reach the destination."[47] I couldn't agree more.

As you move forward, keep insights at the forefront of your strategic planning and decision making. Simply committing to this as a practice can yield significant benefits. Again, opening yourself to new possibilities for innovation and industry disruption will keep you agile and prepared to capitalize on critical, game-changing opportunities.

As important as fostering an environment in which *aha!* moments can occur is remembering that some of the most critical information you can collect will come from your front lines—from conversations with customers and the employees who regularly engage with them. Ultimately, insights are about *people*. About humanity. About the deep-seated emotional attachments that drive any of our pursuits.

A 2010 story about insights from war-torn Colombia helps

---

47   As quoted in Boston Consulting Group, "The Consumer's Voice—Can Your Company Hear It?" BCGPerspectives, accessed September 22, 2017, at https://www.bcgperspectives.com/content/articles/consumer_insight_marketing_consumers_voice/?chapter=4.

make this point. Since 1964, Colombia had been ravaged by war between the national government and the Revolutionary Armed Forces of Colombia (FARC). More than 220,000 Colombians had died, and millions more had been displaced. Then in 2010, in an effort to curb the fighting, the Colombian military hired the Bogotá-based advertising executive José Miguel Sokoloff. And he brokered a peace no one saw coming.

The initial step in Sokoloff's intervention in the conflict was to engage in conversations with anti-government guerilla fighters who hid in the jungle and routinely took civilians and government allies hostage. From his exchanges with them, he gleaned two critical insights.

The first was that a guerilla was as much a prisoner of his own organization as were his hostages. Due to various psychological and logistical constraints, the guerillas Sokoloff interviewed felt they had no way out of the jungle. The second insight was that rebel soldiers consistently reported that their mothers were key influencers of their behavior. Sokoloff's discovery of the rebel soldiers' emotional connection to home combined with his first insight inspired him to architect a campaign to end the decades-long war.

In December 2010, the Colombian military and Sokoloff launched Operation Christmas. In a high-risk operation, they flew deep into rebel territory to decorate nine 75-foot trees near guerilla strongholds. The team installed Christmas lights triggered with motion detectors. Once lit, the trees illuminated banners that read, "If Christmas can come to the jungle, you can come home. Demobilize. At Christmas, everything is possible."

In 2011, the military repeated the campaign. And in 2012, the FARC came to the table to negotiate an end to the war. During the negotiations, guerilla leaders pleaded with the Colombian government to stop the campaign. The government agreed, and in 2016, the parties agreed to a ceasefire.

FINAL NOTE

Whether you're a startup or an industry giant, getting to *aha!* has never been more vital to your success. This mission requires you to learn and listen. It also requires you to empathize with others as you grapple with the discoveries you're bound to make along your journey.

In the end, however, insights' value extends far beyond their capacity to create business success. Insights are visions of what makes us human. They connect us to each other and to the world in which we aspire to live our best lives. In writing this book, I hope I've energized you to consider how you—as a business leader and as an individual—can leverage insights to create better experiences and, ultimately, a better world.

ACKNOWLEDGMENTS

This journey would not have been possible without the unwavering support of my family, colleagues, mentors, and friends. I am grateful to all of you.

A special thanks to my parents, Pinak and Nikki, for encouraging me in all of my pursuits and inspiring me to follow my dreams. I have always known you believe in me and want the best for me.

As for you, the reader, I am grateful our paths have crossed. Thank you, fellow seeker of the *aha!* moment.

ABOUT THE AUTHOR

DARSHAN MEHTA has more than fifteen years of branding, marketing, and insight-strategy experience. In 1998, he pioneered a variety of digital methodologies, including online focus groups and surveys, and founded iResearch, an insights platform that enables companies to quickly and affordably extract insights from consumers worldwide.

Mr. Mehta has also taught at George Washington University in Washington, D.C., University of Gothenburg in Sweden, and Thammasat University in Thailand. Through his work, Mehta has traveled to more than eighty countries and has been published in *Forbes*, *Inc.*, *Entrepreneur*, *The Huffington Post*, *IdeaMensch*, and the *Journal of Advertising Research*.

Learn more at www.gettingtoaha.com.

Made in the USA
Las Vegas, NV
05 November 2021

33735985R00102